LIFE LATER ON

Ann Webber has had over twenty years' experience of working with older people on both residential and community projects. A practising Christian, she has worked for secular as well as religious agencies, including Age Concern England, where she was Head of Training, and the Open University, where she helped to develop two courses for those working with older people. Her last book was *Growing into Fullness: enjoying retirement and old age* (Marshall Pickering, 1986).

Life Later On

OLDER PEOPLE AND
THE CHURCH

Ann Webber

TRI∆NGLE

First published 1990
Triangle
SPCK
Holy Trinity Church
Marylebone Road
London NW1 4DU

British Library Cataloguing in Publication Data
Webber Ann
  Life later on.
  1. Old persons. Social aspects – Christian Viewpoints
  I. Title
  261.83426

ISBN 0–281–04455–4

Typeset by Inforum Typesetting, Portsmouth
Reproduced, printed and bound in Great Britain by
BPCC Hazell Books
Aylesbury, Bucks, England
Member of BPCC Ltd.

Contents

Introduction

Rachel lives alone in a one-bedroom centrally heated flat overlooking a park in the heart of the inner city. She was one of fourteen brothers and sisters, though there are only three of them left now.

Altogether during her seventy-five years she has had five homes – all except the first within a mile of each other. As a child she went to a mission hall and after it closed down during the Second World War moved to the Anglican church where she has been ever since. She's happy there – has lots of friends, runs the afternoon women's fellowship, is on the PCC, acts as a sideswoman and cleans the church every month.

A tiny insight into the life of one elderly lady – and we shall hear her talking more about her life later in the book. This book is about the Rachels, the Emilys, the Johns – each known individually and precious to God. Every church has, or should have, if it reflects the population of its local community, its own Rachels, Emilys, Johns, all individuals, yet most sharing a common heritage. But it is surprising how little is sometimes known about them. It's easy to hold stereotyped views of old age, often unconsciously influenced by the media and story books we had as children – or on the other hand to feel overwhelmed by the fact of their individuality. Many general books about ageing and caring for older people are written each year, but sadly most ignore the spiritual dimension. Yet to grow old as a Christian is a special experience in so many ways.

So perhaps the time has come for church people to take a fresh look at what their older members have to offer and at what God wants us to provide for them, in order that together, we may be lights to the world and be able to share the Christian's knowledge of hope to people who have no hope. As salt in the world, we can show how older people can still be valued and contributing members of the community, however physically frail they may be.

The book is divided into two parts. The first part tackles various experiences that face people in later life: how individuals can be supported; how church communities can use older people's gifts in a more organised way. Part Two focuses on issues of particular concern to church leaders; it gives a biblical framework to old age; briefly looks at some of the more challenging spiritual experiences that God often presents to people and gives suggestions about evangelism amongst older people.

There is no need for you to read from beginning to end. After the first two chapters, dip into the subject areas that concern you most and then return to others later. Share what I say with older people you know. Get their views. This book doesn't aim to provide definitive answers but I hope provides a springboard from which Christians, young and old, can discover a whole new world of rich relationships and through the personal stories a deeper understanding of God himself – he is, after all, the oldest Person who has ever lived!

Part One

CHAPTER 1

Old Age in the Twentieth Century

'I don't feel old. I feel the same as I did twenty years ago.' (*Emily*)

– and yet, how often we hear old people referred to as a problem! Sometimes when I am running seminars about old age I start with a quiz. You might like to try a few of the questions.

1. There will be more old people in Great Britain in the year 2000 than there are today.

   True/False
2. Money is the major concern of people in old age.　　　　　　　　　　　　　　 *True/False*
3. Intelligence declines in old age.　　　 *True/False*
4. Older people are more likely to be the recipients of muggings and other criminal victimisation than other age groups.　　　　　 *True/False*
5. The majority of old people are lonely.

   True/False
6. Older people do not learn as quickly as younger people.　　　　　　　　　　　　 *True/False*
7. Old people are resistant to change.

   True/False

Believe it or not, the answer to each of these questions is: False! There are many reasons why false ideas have arisen. One may stem from the fact that retirement and old age as we know them today are relatively new experiences for our society, so it is only recently that the lives of older people have been studied in depth and general statistics investigated to discover information about old age.

It is important to get the facts about life in later years correct, so that old people's skills and experience can be used imaginatively; attitudes towards them can be realistic; friendship and help can be offered in a way that enables them to grow emotionally and spiritually right to the end of life; and younger generations can view their own old age sensibly. Christians recognise the uniqueness of each individual but a general overview of the attitudes and behaviour of large groups of people can lead to greater understanding of what is normal and what is abnormal. This is particularly true when assumptions are made on the basis of impressions instead of facts. I remember, for instance, some twenty years ago assuming, along with my colleagues, that an eighty-year-old lady must have adjustment problems because she continued her interest in all kinds of community activities. We now know, as a result of research, that people involved in community activities when younger will continue to be so in later years.

Looking at what we know about large groups of people means that their different attitudes and ways can be understood, and what constitutes health can be defined, as can what is psychologically normal and what is abnormal. Properly conducted surveys and research help us to understand how people experience old age and the extent to which the image society tries to portray of them is accurate. Listening to older people talking of their common experience helps to deepen the enjoyment of individual older people and helps others to appreciate the difficulties they face.

But surveys and research can provide only facts. It is up to society to decide whether they will influence how older people are treated. So let us look at the facts.

In 1902 there were about 2.5 million people over sixty-five in Great Britain, whereas in 1984 there were about 10 million – a fourfold increase in eighty years. Many people, now in their eighties, have lived longer than any previous generations of their family (although it is true that living to a 'ripe old age' depends on choosing one's parents carefully!). For the first time in history, most people can automatically expect to live into their retirement years. Never before have there been millions of people who are no longer paid for the work they contribute to society but are financially reclaiming a little of the investment that they have made to society in the past.

Behind the huge rise in the numbers of older people between 1902 and 1984 (but which will now remain steady until the end of the century) lie other issues.

The number of children in families and in the church has dramatically decreased. In 1904, if you surveyed 100 people at random you would find there were:

41 under 19
34 aged 20–39
17 aged 40–59
 8 aged 60 and over

In 1984 there were:

28 under 19
28 aged 20–39

3

    23   aged 40–59
    21   aged 60 and over

But have the churches' ministries changed in
line with this? Do the churches reflect the needs of
the changing numbers of ageing, or even frail
people? In 1900–2 there would have been very few
frail older people, because drugs and treatments
were much more limited. Today three or four in
every hundred people over the age of sixty-five will
be frail and need help in continuing to be active
members of the church. That may sound very few
but let us look at it from the perspective of an
average local community. If a local church ministers to a community of 3000 people there will be
about 630 people over sixty, of whom about twenty are likely either to need help in attending
church-based activities or to require a special kind
of outreach.

The changing balance in the population is also
reflected in the changing age at which death
occurs. In 1902 about 40 per cent of deaths oc-
curred to children under the age of fifteen and
about 34 per cent of death related to people over
sixty-five. By 1982 the picture was very different.
Just under 2 per cent of deaths involved a child
under fifteen whereas 77 per cent of deaths oc-
curred over the age of sixty-five. It may be this fact
that has led to the idea that frailty and old age are
the same thing. In fact this is not true. For most of
the retirement years, the level of independence is
the same as that expected during the previous forty
or fifty years.

The time of frailty and increased dependency,
as at any age, is generally limited to the months
preceding death. There are, of course, some who

experience a long period of frailty but that is true of people in younger age groups as well. However, the length of dependency does gradually lengthen in advanced old age. As death is normally preceded by a period of ill health, and as death is inevitable, there is a tendency to be more aware of frail people than those who are independent even though the latter may be as old, or even older than others.

I was reminded of this the other day when I was walking through the local park with a sprightly, alert man of ninety. Nobody even noticed him, but they did notice the sixty-year-old lady in a wheelchair with arms and legs twisted with the arthritis which she's had for the last twenty years. There is a constant need therefore to make sure we keep things in perspective. Not doing so leads to false stereotypes and wrong attitudes.

Attitudes to Ageing

Another activity I sometimes introduce into seminars is to ask people to make a list of the adjectives and nouns which come to mind as I mention 'old age' or 'elderly people'. Invariably the first words are negative, and it can be ten or fifteen minutes before there are any positive ones. This is sadly not surprising, as society persistently reinforces negative ideas.

You might like to look at some children's books. I asked some young friends of mine, who own about a hundred books, how many of the stories involved old people. They showed me just three – apart from the fairy tales with their stereotyped pictures and stories of old people as witches, magicians, or fairy godmothers. One story is about a young boy going on a miraculous journey with an old magician and an eccentric old lady who dresses up in an array of 'Ascot type' hats. Another is of a grandmother (only in her fifties) who goes on a journey and then loses her memory. The story centres around her young grandson's attempts to find her. The third is an elderly doctor who colludes with a young boy and his poacher father in their rather dubious activities. The doctor is described as white, curly hair and a beard, a genial disposition.

There is also the idea that everyone in retirement must be alike and face the same problems irrespective of age; and yet no one thinks that people of twenty-five and fifty-five are similar – so why think that people in their sixties are the same as people in their nineties?

A prevalent notion in church circles, as well as among many professional workers, is that old people are 'set in their ways' and resistant to change. In fact, from the sixties onwards, people probably have to face more change than during any other time in life. Retirement itself necessitates a completely different lifestyle. Bereavements are experienced far more frequently and can demand enormous adjustments. Ill health requires ingenuity and an ability to adapt to limitations. Studies of retired people repeatedly show that the majority of older people do rise to the challenges presented by these painful events, and are well integrated, mature people.

Another prevalent image is of loneliness in old age, and an assumption that people who live alone are more likely to be lonely than those who share a home with others. In fact this is not true. Recent studies report that loneliness is as likely to be found amongst elderly people who are married or living with other relatives as among those living alone, but that those alone are less ashamed to admit to loneliness. However, the vast majority of elderly people are not lonely, irrespective of their living conditions.

Not long ago I attended a locally scripted amateur pantomime, where the themes were deliberately anti-racist and anti-sexist – yet the elderly fairy godmother, alone among the cast, was portrayed as forgetful and used a walking stick! Another false idea! What actually happens is that young forgetfulness tends to get ignored. Later some of the rationalisations seem increasingly feeble, so new excuses have to be found – getting old becomes a useful peg. In fact unless certain kinds of mental infirmity are present, forgetfulness should not increase, provided minds and brains continue to be regularly stimulated. As with any other part of the body, lack of use leads to deterioration in ability.

The comments I have made so far have been based on clinical and statistical research studies. Much more important are interviews during which old people share their own ideas and experiences. There are now several studies based on many hundreds of older people talking about themselves, as well as assessments of their physical capabilities and how they occupy their time. It is these which have shown what ageist views society holds, and which challenge some deeply held beliefs which I will consider in later chapters.

But there are some issues that are relevant to this background chapter. 1) The older people become the more they feel able to manage on the money they have, even though the older they are the lower their income is likely to be. 2) With increasing age good health becomes increasingly important – and more important than money. 3) Good friends and neighbours are deeply appreciated, as is 4) the ability to be content with life; and that reminded me of Paul's words which were written in a Roman prison – 'I have learned in whatever state I am to be content.' 5) Amongst younger retired people a happy marriage is also rated very highly. 6)The amount of frailty is much lower than might be imagined, with less than 3 per cent of elderly people considering themselves permanently housebound or bedfast and over 90 per cent able to go out unassisted.

Not surprising a major cause of low morale is a feeling of not being important to anyone. Ironically, as Christians we have probably contributed to that feeling in older people, by over-emphasis on the 'giving' nature of Christianity rather than its 'reciprocity'. This is sad, because love is the foundation principle of life, and always requires us to be as willing to receive from others as to give to them. When we refuse to allow older people to give, we deny them the opportunity to express love.

Older People's Biographies

Today it is recognised that a changing culture affects lifestyles, and indeed in neighbourhoods where people from many nations live, this is experienced daily. What is easy to forget, is the extent to which British society has changed since 1900 – in family structures, educational opportunities, technological changes, the role of women, mobility, to name a few. Older people have lived through these changes and in this sense have a common biography even though the effect the changes will have had on each person will be unique.

It is worth reading books or looking at documentaries on television about life in town, country and city in the years before you were born, and about the big events which affected everyone deeply – like the wars, the depression of the 1930s, farm mechanisation, emigration policies, and the comparative affluence of the post-Second World War years. These provide a broad framework for the understanding of older people's background. But it must never be forgotten that it is the personal history that counts most – where we were born; how we were brought up; the numbers of brothers and sisters, nephews, nieces, grandchildren; whether we are married or remain single; our first car, motorcycle, job. So every person's story has common threads with others and yet is unique – and it becomes more and more individual with age.

Rachel, who I wrote about at the beginning of the book, shared other parts of her story with me. Here are some extracts:

Like all my brothers and sisters I was born at home. Father scraped together the money for the midwife and she provided the sheets and blankets for the first month. But actually I was born on straw. Soon after I was born (I'm the youngest) we moved to London to a flat with three rooms. We collected water in a bucket from the tap in the yard and boiled it on a black lead stove heated by a coal fire. When it came to bathing all the boys went into another room while the girls bathed and then the girls left the room while the boys had their turn. Mum said the boys got dirtier so the girls should be done first . . .

All of us had jobs to do, and because I was a girl I soon had to help with ironing, but Mum only gave me the dark-coloured clothes because I kept scorching things – we had to heat the iron on the stove and I never could guess the heat right . . .

In 1928 one of my brothers emigrated to Canada. Mum was very upset but Dad said, 'Good luck! If I was your age I'd do it'. In 1930 another went to Australia. I'm still in touch with those nieces and nephews but Fred and Betty, Bill and Florrie have passed on . . .

We didn't get through the depression too badly. Dad was a cobbler and shoes always need mending. I was lucky, soon after I left school in 1926 and the general strike finished, I got a job as a thread trimmer. It was a real sweat shop, still it was a job. It kept me in London during the war years – we made the shirts and blouses for the troops and land girls. At night we spent the time in the shelter at St Agnes church. In the morning when I went to work I had to climb over all the people sleeping on the underground platforms to get on the tube.

At first Mum wouldn't come to the shelter, but after a while she wouldn't leave it even during the day. She got really scared after our flat was damaged by a bomb. Then we found a small house and Mum died there in 1952. Since then I've been alone. Gradually everyone was moved out of our street but I never heard anything. Then one day when I came home from work I found my doorway bricked up. 'Oh,' said the workmen, 'We didn't think anyone lived here.' So they took the bricks out. Finally, a few months later they gave me this flat.

It's nice and warm but the neighbours aren't the same. When I was young the people next door always came in and out and we were always in there. They were like family. Not like today when you're supposed to keep your door locked. Mrs — next door is always telling me off for leaving my front door open . . .

A short précis of part of one person's life. Rachel enjoys talking about her experiences, and the children at the nearby school invite her to their class when they are doing local history lessons.

Life has been tough for Rachel as it has been for millions of others of today's elderly people, yet she doesn't dwell on it. She has lots of friends, particularly at church, and takes a lively interest in all that goes on there.

Other people will have other experiences. Many will have spent the '20s and '30s nursing fathers and brothers who were gassed in the First World War. Others will have lost fathers and brothers in that war. Like Rachel, others saw relatives emigrating in the '20s and '30s. Life was hard, the general strike of 1926 and the depression through the early 1930s affected most working class families. Then came the 1939–45 war and its disruption to family life; again brothers and fathers were killed in action. It was not until 1954 that rationing finally ended. Prosperity was growing; many more people bought their own homes on mortgages; city councils built vast estates, compulsorily moving thousands of people; the motor car became a familiar sight;

holidays and outings became the norm rather than the 'special treats' of the past; television brought the world into people's dining or sitting rooms. And so technology and wealth continue to change people's lives.

Some Psychological Views on Ageing

At one level all this has made life today a very different experience from that of any previous generation. However, the way in which each person reacts to the challenge that comes from these experiences is probably not so different.

Each person reaches old age with a unique biography: a unique basic personality which can be seen even at birth, even as we can see the distinct physical characteristics; a temperament that has been reinforced or changed by thousands of experiences throughout the whole of life; an intellectual ability set to some extent in younger years but influenced by the many educational opportunities of adulthood; emotional maturity which has been affected as much by class and cultural influences as by the personal handling of life events.

All this will affect the way a person approaches the special challenges of later life, as will the attitudes, the social roles and the facilities (or lack of them) that society makes available to them. Back in the 1950s the usual professional view of old age was that it should be a time when people become more preoccupied with themelves and less concerned about the outside world. It was seen as a time when people prepared for death and took on no new responsibilities or challenges.

Slowly many people came to see the falseness of this picture and inevitably there was a swing to the opposite extreme. The idea then was that 'successful' ageing depended on continued social involvement, and that needs didn't change in old age. Any decline in social contact should be resisted.

But the 1950s' view has for some people continued to be the popular one. The result, and I have seen it too often for comfort, can be that people when they retire begin to play the dependent passive role – usually with considerable difficulty at first, but gradually the acting becomes easier – until that way of behaving becomes a way of life. Lethargy, apathy and purposelessness result – depression is not uncommon.

The danger of the opposite view is that retired people can be encouraged to fill their days as fully as previously, to ignore their past, to feel guilty if they spend a lot of time relaxing and to feel that they are failures if or when frailty comes.

Another idea encountered in certain types of counselling is based on what is called 'life span development'. It takes a very negative view of old age, seeing a person's problems totally in terms of loss, and how people cope purely in terms of their experiences in very early life. It ignores adult experiences, the depth of current relationships, the person's own views about their life in retirement and their contribution to society. Yet most of us who are experienced in the field of ageing would bear out older people's own view that these latter factors have a crucial influence on their ability to age successfully.

This theory also suggests that mistakes made earlier in life can rarely be corrected, and it does not acknowledge the existence of sin. It therefore inevitably clashes with the teaching of Jesus about salvation, forgiveness and the constant opportunities for new life and growth that God can give everyone at every age.

The idea has never been systematically researched to prove whether it has any truth. But that also applies to several other ideas that are being studied at present.[1] However, looking at ageing from a variety of secular viewpoints can help to increase our understanding – providing we recognise that they all have severe limitations. But that is what makes getting to know people exciting – they cannot be neatly labelled as a group, or given prescriptive solutions to their problems; nor do we need to have preconceived ideas about our own old age!

Where Does the Church Fit In?

If you know some of the older people in your church, what I have written about Rachel will ring bells. But if you don't, why not start to discover their stories?

Enjoying the company of older people does not require any special skills. Old people are no different from young people – as Emily, quoted at the beginning of this chapter, said to me: 'I don't feel old . . .' but they do obviously have far more experience of life and therefore far more to give. The church should allow them to share their knowledge and to give their skills. They are part of the body of Christ.

To get to know somebody involves letting them talk about themselves – their experience of life, the traditions they have known and what is important to them. Some possible ways of starting to get to know older people more deeply are to ask them about their experiences of the war, the depression,

14

outings and holidays, school and the games they played, marriage, work, children, what the later part of life was like for their parents, especially if they were old when they died. Personal questions should obviously be avoided, but one or two open-ended questions will usually open up fascinating discussions. Most people enjoy talking about their past. Meeting old friends usually leads to reminiscence; talking to younger people has the same function. If you are apprehensive about starting, or not sure what it might feel like, seek out some teenagers and get them to ask you about your memories.

Tell older people about your own past so that it is a sharing of experiences you have in common. I know of no better way of having one's prejudices demolished. A minister once said, 'Generally we only minister to the last two or three years, when there is a lifetime of experience.' Older people have enormous experience of solving personal problems and this will gradually come out as they talk. Learning from them can widen younger people's experience of how to cope and solve difficulties; and older people can usefully be linked with people who need help with a similar problem. For example I have known several occasions when an elderly person who had lost a child has been able to help a young mum coping with similar tragedy.

Knowing and understanding how a person views their past enables them and us to identify their strengths and weaknesses. So often they can be encouraged to cope with a current problem by remembering how they coped on a similar occasion in the past.

Talking with people like Rachel always makes

me feel very humble. To hear how they have overcome appalling problems and coped under pressure always increases my respect and gives me a
deepened wish to encourage them when they face
new challenges. For those who are constant grum-
blers and who have given in, I gain a new compassion that knows that but for God's grace the same
things could happen to me. Love demands that we
open ourselves to people so that they can love us.
Within the Church there is no place for professional relationships – love demands that we both give
and take. We are equal.

CHAPTER 2

Spiritual Dimensions to Ageing

Society's views about ageing are usually negative and the various psychological theories are to a large extent academic and do not really tie up with what older people say. This gives us, as Christians, a marvellous opportunity to bring a distinctly biblical perspective to growing older and to society's attitudes – and the Bible has lots to say about that period of life!

The Biblical Perspectives

In Part Two of this book I give more biblical detail, but here I want to summarise some of the main issues as I see them. The Bible documents cover many hundreds of years and involve a number of different cultures. Yet behind it all there exist themes that are just as relevant to us today as they were when they were first written.

A recurring theme is that long life comes through obeying God's laws. This is because obedience leads to peace and harmony, not only within each person, but also between people; on a wider scale this leads to long life through the absence of wars – a major cause of death in biblical times. One reason for the numbers of old people in Britain decreasing since 1986 is the number of men who died in the 1939–45 war.

Another biblical theme is respect for older people. Hebrew society doubtless did not find that easy, any more than we do – otherwise we would not find a command to honour father and mother in the Ten Commandments, as well as other references in both the Old and New Testaments. On the other hand, in some cultures old people can be idealised as 'the wise', although the proverb in Ecclesiastes 4.13 points out that that isn't always true.

Physically handicapped people of all ages are accustomed to being constantly ignored although they are quite capable of speaking for themselves. In the Bible we have many stories of elderly, physically frail people still using their faculties to the full. Age and frailty did not mean that people should be put in a corner out of the way. It's interesting to note how specific the Bible is about the capacities and incapacities of individuals. Are we as specific in our attitudes to older people?

There is also another principle – most clearly set out by Paul – that we should always be seeking to grow into all the fullness of God. The Bible never tells us that we can cease from seeking a deeper union with God when we get old. Do we expect older people to continue to grow as Christians? Do we ourselves expect to go on growing until the end of our lives? Not that growing will be easy. We only have to read Psalm 71 to see the struggle that that writer experienced. Yet all the promises of God are as valid for old age as they are at any other.

I believe that underlying the issues I have raised there is another biblical principle – that every person is equal in God's sight. I am always excited by the fact that the records we have of Jesus' birth tell us that he met then both old and young; and on the Day of Pentecost Peter quotes Joel's prophecy with its emphasis on equality and inclusiveness (see Chapter 11, p. 153).

Old age provides a time of supreme opportunity, but it may also be a time of painful testing.

The past experiences of life often need to be looked at, wrong things confessed, people who have been hurt and done wrong to, forgiven and blessed, good things rejoiced over; so that God's hand is seen at work and life can be recognised as a tapestry and not as a jumble of threads of wool; new experiences need to be added to all that has gone before. Not everyone can do all this without help – particularly if a hard life has led to bitterness and resentfulness. Those who have come to faith in God late in life may need a special kind of help.

As at all ages it is the shared friendship, the gentle nurturing of faith through all its phases of development and the willingness to work with God at his speed, that is essential if someone is to be brought to a living faith. Those whom God dramatically rescues are very few – though especially in a crisis his way may be speedy. There is certainly a need to continue to preach the gospel to older people in a way they can understand and which meets their needs.

After a person has accepted the way of Christ many memories may need dealing with, and we need to be very sensitive to what God is doing as the pain and other feelings come out. It is important to remember that many of today's older people were taught a very one-sided view of religion and personal feelings. I have several books on my shelf, written in the 1940s, and highly recommended in their day, which suggested that feelings are not important, or even worse, should be ignored. This teaching will often tend to catch up on people, and then the feelings may come out in ways that are not obvious – from hardness of heart to physical illness. There is a delicate balance to achieve between ignoring our feelings, acknowledging our true feelings even when they are unpleasant or bad, and paying too much attention to them. No generation seems to have got the balance right – probably because it must be an individual balance and should change according to what issues the person is facing. Older, well integrated Christians can have much to share and teach about all this.

Jane, now aged seventy-eight, shared with me how she had become a Christian and what her faith means to her now.

I went to Sunday school at my mother's and grandmother's church – I don't remember anything except that my sister and I played games all the way through. My father went to the Methodists because he was a good singer and they had a well known choir.

I occasionally went to church whilst I was training to be a nurse but one day thought, 'Why am I going; I'm just as good as they are.' So I stopped . . .

Father died during the war and I went back to nurse my mother with pneumonia. But I got rheumatic fever and was ill in bed for a few months. Then a friend of my sister's asked if I would like to go and convalesce with her in the country. She was a Baptist and talked to me a lot. When I went back to London I got baptised. People started commenting on my patience but I gradually gave up going to church – it's difficult when you're a private agency nurse. I was forced to retire at fifty-five because of ill health and I finally managed to get a filing job which I hated – and with a sigh of relief I finally retired at sixty. I started going to church . . .

I love the Bible. I read it every morning and evening and it helps. The Bible reading notes, *Every Day with Jesus*, go to the point every day. I often read the Psalms out loud. I love the New Testament, especially the letters. I started with the King James. It's beautiful but I wanted something easier to understand so I used J.B. Phillips, then the Living Bible, then the New English Bible and now the New International Version. But I'm talking to God all day, and that's growing, and if anything happens to disturb my morning time I miss it frightfully. Both the talking and the silence are growing all the time. Often I'm sitting in bed getting ready to pray and then it happens – I'm lost. It is companionship with him.

A few weeks back life was very dark. I felt that God wasn't anywhere. I sat down and began to feel guilty and I knew I had hidden something from him. It lasted two or three days; then it dawned on me what was wrong. Having discovered what it was, I put it right and all was then OK. God is such a comfort. When I get so worried, I can't talk properly. It ends in tears while I'm still trying to say it. And it all turns out all right very soon. He's amazing. He's so near all the time.

I have a picture in my mind now. Jesus standing just there with a peaceful look. Sometimes he says, 'Don't worry', – or a couple of words. Sometimes 'Do this or that'. I often say to Jesus, 'I can't go out evangelising but I want you to shine through me' . . .

Now he's teaching me more about patience – not waiting – a different kind. I've a special friend who's had a very hard life but she's very temperamental. She's had an awful lot of trouble and pours it out on the phone for an hour at a time. I have to try not to scream. When I got ill I had to say to God, 'I cannot take any more. God, how can I cope? Please give me patience.' Gradually it worked and she's improved. People have always poured out their troubles to me and now I know what to say. Now I can't be so active I like to visit people ill in hospital – I can bring them God's comfort . . .

I've something that's always bothered me. If someone tried to hurt me I could turn the other cheek, but if someone tried to hurt my family I couldn't. I haven't got an answer to that one yet . . .

Jane is continuing to grow as a Christian and it is easy to see how her prayer pattern has shifted over the years. The slowing pace of life gives God the opportunity. As prayer is not so worried, it becomes more reflective. For some, like Jane, there is more silence, prayer usually becomes much deeper and there is a greater harmony with the Spirit. But each new depth often involves struggle, loneliness or emptiness. A life of prayer in old age is not a soft option. Christians from an evangelical background whom God moves down this path often find it difficult and strange to cope with. They are used to a much more verbal form of prayer, in which answers are seen through ordinary circumstances of church and life. It seems to me, too, that intercession becomes more the seeking of God's will on how to pray rather than telling God about the circumstances.

This is of course not true for all people. Our God is a God of diversity. Those whose experience of prayer has been anchored in and based on church prayer meetings may experience little change perhaps, until frailty prevents them from attending prayer meetings. The problems that can then occur are mentioned in a later chapter.

As life becomes less pressured, so there is the chance for everything that is done, at the time it is done, to become a conscious, continual offering to God, and this in turn can become a life which is endless prayer; a constant union with God himself. Jane is striving for this. Ideally, of course, it is how everyone should live life all the time, at all ages, but as Brother Lawrence, in *The Practice of the Presence of God*, has so graphically portrayed, it is not easy. The hectic bustle of working life, the need for strict routines usually worked out under pressure, hinder the attempts. Yet the purpose of life is union with God in working out his purpose in his world which he created. Old age is a time when this purpose can be worked out more deeply.

Older People and Religion

To consider how God views old age is essential if people are to be encouraged to take a biblical, and therefore healthy, attitude towards it. If the gospel is to be preached sensitively as well as realistically then there also needs to be an awareness of older people's possible attitudes to God and to religion. These will be influenced by the teaching they received about God in earlier years, and by each person's own individual experience of life.

Little detailed research has been done into people's attitude to religion at any age, and the

23

information about older people is conflicting. However it seems that possibly over 50 per cent of older people regularly watch or listen to religious programmes on television and radio, have a faith of some kind and consider themselves as members of a particular denomination. One study suggests that religion becomes more important to many people as they grow old.[1]

Although drawing on personal experience can be dangerous, I have known quite a number of people over the years who became practising Christians in old age. Older people's attitudes to religion are influenced by the contact they have had with churchgoing people throughout their lives. Inevitably there will be the horror stories, and these need to be talked through, and there may be the need to repent on behalf of our brethren.

Many older people find modern worship difficult, even though most accept that the change was inevitable and rarely complain or grumble. Those who are younger and who are accustomed to constant change can only dimly understand just what it can mean to have things which have been done for centuries – and which were expected to continue for centuries – suddenly dismissed or, even worse, scorned and despised. Yet many of today's older people (including the middle aged!) grew up with the King James Bible being considered the authoritative Word of God; with an acutely developed sense of God's 'otherness'; with hymns which remained unchanged for years; and for Roman Catholics and Anglicans in particular, services which were marked with dignity and simple splendour. That has all changed within a short time span – we now have a multitude of Bible translations, many using simple words; there is more informality and intimacy in public prayer; a plethora of new hymns and choruses sung at a speed which defies clear pronunciation and understanding; services which are unrecognisable to the liturgically minded. Added to that are the liberal and neo-orthodox theologies which have replaced the unquestioning authority of the Bible, which so often have now permeated down to local congregations, whereas in earlier days religious controversies rarely affected the 'person in the pew'.

Behind all this is the inference that what happened and what was taught in the past is all wrong. It is not surprising that some older people are confused; others feel their faith threatened and react accordingly; and others feel they are unwanted and their experience of God worthless. Although many react with incredible maturity, some can only cope by clinging tightly to what is left of the past; others through experiencing this crisis of faith reject God; others just retreat into the background. The church as a result is the poorer. Yet the God of their youth and younger years is still the same God. Older people's understanding of God needs to be accepted and listened to if the aspects of his character that he is reminding us of today are to be correctly understood. Then the next generation can in its turn understand, in context, God's new revelation to them. If today's older people's experience of God is ignored, future generations cannot be expected to believe that today's knowledge of God has any relevance for them. History will repeat itself.

How Can Other Christians Help?

A recurring theme throughout this book is the major need in older pepole to feel that they are valued and can still give to others. Unlike technological knowledge, which becomes out of date within a few years, spiritual knowledge and experience can never date. Older people, therefore, have much to share. But they need to be approached with humility – and at the point of their personal experience. Starting points can be reading and discussing Bible passages together; asking them about the way God and Jesus were portrayed when they were younger, and what they learned from that; what the church was like when they were young; how faith in Jesus was preached; how the changes have come. Gradually, areas where they have come to a balance through struggle will become obvious and these may be the points at which their advice can be sought on how others can resolve similar difficulties.

As older people realise that they have things to contribute from experience they will gradually open up on the deeper challenges that are facing them. They may find it difficult at first to share deep spiritual problems, because they come from a generation when personal dilemmas were not shared. But life is about constantly adapting and responding to new challenges, and this does not stop in old age. God is always leading his people onward and upwards.

Crises of faith will continue, and new ways of coping and growing will need to be explored. Help in discerning God's will, and people to stand alongside when the battle is particularly bad, bring encouragement. It is not always easy to stand alongside. Sometimes it involves us facing fears about old age in ourselves. Sometimes it is difficult really to understand what the older person is thinking or saying – their way of life may have been so different from our own. But God does enable understanding if his help is specifically asked for. A person may be facing something for which none of their previous experience has prepared them, and they feel lonely or afraid. The changes in the interpretation of theology and all the other changes mentioned earlier, do sometimes have a profound effect on one's faith. God may seem very far away, and coping with life without the awareness of God is perhaps one of the greatest spiritual battles anyone ever has to face.

People who are undergoing this experience need a lot of support to keep holding on. They may have less physical energy, and some may be afraid of giving in. Others become bitter or resentful, and it takes a lot of time, patience, love and encouragement to help someone like this to admit their feelings honestly. To recognise that God's love is limitless and not dependent on any personal effort, worthiness, achievements or failures, self-understanding or anything else, never comes without a struggle – it is God's freely given unmerited grace. Such recognition leads to humility, which is a hallmark of spiritual growth. But the Church must not take advantage of that humility. The quiet, unassuming presence of an older person needs to be recognised for what it is, and these people should not be ignored or their gifts left unnoticed and unused. To do so not only devalues them, but it will hamper their spiritual growth. It will also make it more difficult for them to accept their own fundamental worth.

CHAPTER 3

Retirement – A Time for New Growth

'Every branch that does bear fruit he [the Father] prunes, that it may bear more fruit.' (John 15.2)

So said Jesus in his high priestly teaching in John 15. Whenever there are new experiences, something has to be relinquished in order that what is new can be embraced. But most people tend to find any change in life and circumstances difficult, and the adjustment takes time. This is true even if the change is looked forward to. (Take marriage for example. It is natural to be excited at its prospect and there is the longing to be sharing life with one's partner, but the early period of living together involves adjustments which are often painful.) Therefore the adjustment to retirement from work is not likely to be accomplished in a few days. This is true whether retirement is welcomed as a reprieve from a mind-destroying routine nine-to-five job, or whether it is regretted because the job has been stimulating and rewarding. But there is much that can be done to ease transition.

Ideally, financial planning should have started as early in life as the twenties and thirties and be reviewed again in the mid-forties and fifties, in order to lessen the financial effects of retirement. New interests can be taken up in mid-life that will meet more limited financial circumstances and at least one interest can be chosen that can be pursued if and when failing health should come. Having a balanced attitude to health and exercise in younger years will mean that it is easier to keep fit in later life.

If friendships with people of all ages are maintained and enjoyed in younger life then that will continue and strengthen as the inevitable loss of older friends and relatives is faced. If retirement is prepared for, when it comes it will be less of an upheaval.

Our elders of today have not had these advantages. Until recently, there were few schemes which enabled people to provide financially for old age, apart from the state pension, and there was little or no talk of preparing for retirement. Even today, retirement courses are rare and except for those arranged by employers they mainly attract people who have recently retired. In previous generations fewer people lived into old age and therefore there was less interest in studying the effects of retirement and how to ease them.

Is Adjusting to Retirement Difficult?

But you may feel that the retired people you know don't seem to have any problems. When I gave the subject headings of this book to one pastor for comment, he replied that the chapter on retirement could be left out because 'a high proportion of those who have retired have thought the matter out very well and usually end up with a declared philosophy, 'I don't know however I found time to go out to work!'

What is your experience? Has everyone you've known found the change easy? If you have not known many people, you might like to seek the views of retired members of your church.

My own experience is that unless people are intending to switch to other full time employment or time-consuming voluntary activity, adjustment is not easy, and that the challenge comes in major areas:

1. saying goodbye to a large part of one's life, the relationships that go with it, and looking and planning for the future;
2. suddenly finding an extra eight to ten hours available each day, and having to be responsible for ordering one's own life;
3. working on changed relationships within the family, and longer-term relationships;
4. coping with economic changes.

Let's look at each of the four areas in turn.

Leaving regular employment

Although there are now large numbers of unemployed, as a society there still is a tendency to measure an individual's status by the work they do. I find it fascinating, when being introduced to someone, to see how long it is before I am asked what I do for a living – rarely is it longer than a couple of minutes. Christians often unwittingly overstress the value of work. This is perhaps less true now than in the past, but we need to remember that people retiring now will have become conditioned to that attitude over the years.

Retirement from work will therefore present a whole range of challenges, depending on how people have seen the role of work in their lives.

There will be the 'workaholics', who have allowed their jobs to provide all their pleasure and security. Others may have retreated into their work from an unhappy marriage or home situation. For others, work may have been the means of developing personal gifts and skills and have been very satisfying because of its creativity. For others, although the work may have been repetitious, the friendship and cameraderie has given them a sense of belonging and self-esteem. Others, though, may have felt oppressed by repetitive work and an unhappy working atmosphere. Yet others, particularly in physically stressful or strenuous occupations, may be looking forward to a less exhausting life. Yet others may have developed other interests alongside their work – and this will be particularly true of those involved in the life of a church and who have a commitment to God. Nevertheless, everyone will experience a similar range of feelings although of varying intensity according to their individual sensitivity, their attitude to retirement, and the value they place on the work they have done.

Whilst preparing this book I talked with John Frost who retired from his job as works manager for a small family firm. He told me:

> I used to look forward to my retirement, and after forty years received my pension. All the senior employees came up to the boardroom and the managing director thanked me for my years of service and everyone clapped. Suddenly, as I was going down in the lift I felt a strange emptiness and anxiety. Everything seemed different. I didn't have a place any more. The next Monday morning I didn't have a reason for getting up.
>
> I suppose it took me about two months to begin to sort myself out, and about a year before I felt free and happy again.

John is a mature, well balanced man, able to recognise and acknowledge his feelings. He has a cheerful disposition and his sense of achievement in his job and life generally has gradually over the years enabled him to develop the new interests he had planned. He has also discovered an artistic streak which has given him a creative outlet. Work being cut out of his life has already resulted in much new fruit – but not without pain and struggle.

The emptiness that John speaks about is a common feeling – there is the sudden realisation that here is a situation which has not been experienced before, and that the well-tried methods of coping do not meet the need. The filling of the gaps – or the new growth where work has been pruned out – can only come with time. At first, people can be helped by having others to whom they can express their feelings and bewilderment. They may find themselves behaving in a way that is out of character, such as getting short tempered when they are usually placid and patient. They then need reassurance that this is normal and only a passing phase. Time is necessary.

Some people plan ahead for the first few months of retirement – perhaps a world cruise, re-ordering the garden, redecorating the house. The emptiness can then come once these jobs are completed – sometimes with greater force because it is unexpected.

But the situation can be very different for someone whose whole life has been wrapped up in their job. Then the sense of emptiness and isolation may be very frightening indeed, and they will have more problems in working out a new life for themselves.

To some extent everyone behaves differently in different circumstances – individual temperaments and varieties of situations draw out different sides of the personality. There is nothing wrong with that. But sometimes situations arise where instead of being natural, people act a part; their behaviour in one setting conflicts with their behaviour in another. When a person's true character is primarily worked out through their employment and they 'act' a role at home and/or in the church, then their sense of self-esteem frequently becomes very badly damaged on retirement.

Then too, work will for some people have given them an unhealthy state of power and authority.

Maggie Wright was an accounts clerk, who was responsible for the employees' wages, which meant that she knew a lot about people's personal circumstances. It gave her a sense of power. Likewise at church, where she was a deacon, she always felt it her responsibility to know as much as possible about everyone else. 'If I know, I can pray', she would say. After her retirement her nosiness got gradually worse, as having time on her hands she began weaving fantasies around what she did find out and in order to try to prove her worth gossiped: 'I know you pray, so can you pray about . . .'

But emptiness through pruning can be the point of new growth. It is an opportunity for people to look at the gifts they have, some of which may have been buried since childhood, and to think through how they can use them in new ways. Retirement can then bring about a more integrated and harmonious life. Again and again, Paul talks about the aim of each person's life being union with Christ; and oneness with him does not come unless there is unity within oneself. Also, it is when people are able to be their true selves wherever they are that they can be most open to others and God can use them most fully. The 'new fruit' in retirement can be ever more abundant.

Those who retire from work gradually, or who make their retirement plans years ahead and arrange for 'spare time' activities to become more important, may experience no sense of emptiness – it may feel just like a 'job change'. But at all stages of life there is the need for a sense of purpose, a sense of meaning, and this is no less true in retirement than at other times.

Time

It is easy to be unaware of how much of our time is taken up with work. You might like to make out a timetable for the last week for yourself, or your husband, or someone you know well who spends the major part of the weekdays earning money. Then draw up a revised timetable showing the 'free time' that retirement would bring. It is not only the actual working hours that are affected, but there is also the travelling time, time for 'unwinding', and possible television time which is the result of a 'hard day's work'. Habit and routine provide a sense of security – in one day most of this disappears. It is not surprising that some people feel lost, others 'fill up' all the hours with other things as quickly as possible, whilst still others who have never belonged to any sort of club or organisation, church or secular, drift into sitting in front of the television all day. Freedom can be a frightening experience. Retirement gives new freedoms.

The Bible teaches us that to be healthy each person needs both a deep relationship with God – prayer – and deep relationships with other people.

There is the need to give time to oneself and time to others. The balance between these different demands – time for God, others, self – will vary for each person, and at different times in life. All are necessary for spiritual, emotional, mental and physical wholeness.

The value of each human being in God's eyes lies in the fact that he has personally created each person. Work has been part of his plan for everyone since the time of creation when he gave mankind 'dominion . . . over every living thing that moves upon the earth' (Genesis 1.26). We can be sure, then, that God has his vision of how the later years of each person can be used for his glory. The later stages of life bring the opportunity to think afresh of how our God given gifts can be used.

Today there are many opportunities for serving other people and for meeting community and environmental needs; and books written for retired people usually identify some. There is a reasonably comprehensive list of possible activities in Appendix B. There is a difference between hobbies and service to the community and the church – although sometimes the two will overlap. Time spent on oneself is a source of enjoyment when it is complemented by other things, but day after day spent knitting for oneself or doing the garden (unless it is exceptionally large) soon loses its attraction.

Relationships

A common experience when someone retires is for workmates to encourage the retired person to go back and see them. The person takes up the invitation and sees that his place has been taken by someone else, that they are getting on very well without him; or he arranges to meet his old work-mates at the pub they've all gone to on a Friday night after work. He slowly finds he can enter into the conversation less and less as they talk about issues which they have all been involved in whereas he has not; new people are employed – their names mean nothing to him, and gradually he feels more and more shut out and separated from them. This loss of closeness often triggers memories of earlier friendships and relationships. This can be an enjoyable experience when they have been rich and rewarding; but the memories can also be frightening. It means facing and accepting failures as well as the successes.

When failures outweigh successes it is easy to become demoralised, to feel worthless, to feel that our life has been wasted. Where there is a sense of success then there is more likely to be optimism about the future.

Sometimes work has been a means of someone escaping from facing the negative side of their character (as with Maggie Wright), and even using work as a justification for their negativity.

The person who has always found it difficult to accept or understand themselves may have special challenges to face and overcome. Wise care and support can allow the person to grow and change if they so wish.

Marriage Relationships. Retirement demands a lot of adjustment between married partners. When the wife has been at home, and the children have either left home or are at work all day, she may well have become involved with activities in or for the church and community. She will in any event have a well running routine. All that suddenly changes.

New routines have to be established, based on how much the partners want to do together or alone. Meals need to be fixed for new times. It may not be as easy to fit in activities like coffee mornings or women's meetings.

The couple will spend much more time together so that they will both require a greater degree of tolerance and patience than previously. The retiring person will hope to get extra reassurance and comfort from the other as he/she works out a new life for themselves. They will need to feel as valued for their intrinsic worth as they have thought they were for their job and income. Where the marriage has been close, a new depth can come through this difficult time. Each can, through their oneness of spirit, discover new sides of their own and their partner's character. Each, when they have God in the first place in their lives, can move to a new level of acceptance of the other and their idiosyncracies, a new serenity and a deeper contentment. Communication is the all-important key.

But where the marriage has been less than harmonious the change will bring new strains. Patience and tolerance are often at a premium anyway. The willingness to give, take and understand has already taken a severe knocking. Communication skills are likely to be in short supply. Some marriages break altogether at this point, but most couples find some way of coping, albeit a less than satisfactory one.

Another problem can arise when the wife is resistant to adjusting her way of life. She has a settled routine – washing, ironing, shopping, cooking, cleaning – that has served well for years. She has her own network of friends and social outlets. For the woman whose life has been her home, her husband's retirement can come as an unwelcome intrusion. This can make the husband, who now wants to give more time and energy to their home, feel rejected, shut out and perhaps of little value. The wife for her part feels threatened, her job and role coming under scrutiny; she was probably happy with her lifestyle. At such times other couples who have been retired a little longer can be supportive of the newly retired. They know what it is like at first hand.

Singleness. For those who are single or widowed, many friendships made through work may fade out – the cost of travelling, different interests, and so on, gradually drawing the couple apart – but other friendships may blossom and new companionships develop.

The single person particularly needs to be aware of the necessity to remain actively involved in life. A couple have mutual responsibilities the one to the other. The single person may have none. Retirement can bring amazing freedom of service – after all they probably have few ties – but again it takes time to work it out. A person may feel a sense of purposelessness which leads to depression, and church friends in particular need to help them recognise that they are a very important part of the church community. They may need help to catch the vision of their home, skills, freedom being used creatively.

Economic Changes

Financially, life for a retired person may feel more restricted. There is the inevitable cut in income and any future improvement in circumstances is unlikely. The retirement pension will probably continue to rise roughly in line with inflation, and some people are fortunate enough to also have an occupational pension which may increase a little each year. Many, though, will be dependent on income from savings, and a minority on income support. Some older people live in areas where free or subsidised public transport is available, others may avail themselves of other concessionary benefits available to pensioners, but others live or retire in isolated rural communities where bus fares are expensive.

Many books about the financial aspects of retirement have been written but the situation is complicated, so it is best to consult recently published books at the local library as the need arises.

But like the other aspects of retirement, getting used to a lower income takes time, even if there is a generous pension. For many people their income will be very limited and churches need to be sensitive to this when making appeals for money. It may be appropriate sometimes for a person to think in terms of giving service rather than money; for example a retired secretary may be able to deal with correspondence, administration, etc., instead of the church employing a paid church administrator. Sensitivity to individual circumstances is essential.

How Can Christians Help?

It will be clear from what I have said that there is the constant temptation to value ourselves and each other for what we *do* rather than for what we *are*. Where people have fallen into this trap changes in life like retirement can lead to a loss of self-worth. They need to be helped to continue to value themselves and recognise afresh their preciousness in the sight of God. Christian friends can encourage them by ensuring that they are drawn into appropriate activities; asking how things are going, and being willing to spend time with them if they want to talk in more depth.

People need the opportunity to express their feelings – some of which may be unexpected, others new and unpleasant. Frequently the feelings will be ones which are difficult to face because they are painful or sinful. However, acknowledgement is the first step in repentance, and God's forgiveness and freedom cannot come without it. It is important to recognise that some people, who find change difficult or who are insecure, may become very tense and may be generally more difficult to live with. This provides a good opportunity for a lesson in patience!

Helping people to discover and use their gifts within the church and community will require prayer, and maybe imaginative thinking. For some people it will be a question of them continuing to use their work skills, for others it will be developing new ones or re-using old ones. It can often be an opportunity for the church to reach the local community in a new way. A retired accountant or solicitor could perhaps hold a session once a week or fortnight to help ordinary people with basic financial or legal difficulties; a retired teacher might start an after school club; or help youth club members who are having difficulty in getting jobs. Others might be able to undertake door-to-door evangelism. The opportunities are endless. But the retired person will need to analyse his or her skills – are they practical (carpentry, cake making, handicrafts) and/or intellectual (financial, writing) and/or 'emotional' (listening, caring for people)? Sometimes people unwittingly infer that someone who has just retired from work will also wish to relinquish posts of responsibility in the church. Generally this is the worst possible time for that to happen; although of course sometimes it is what God wants, and then the person will know that it is right.

Listening to people, sharing their stories as they sort things out, can be a valuable pastoral ministry at this time. Savour with them their achievements, be encouraged by their triumphs over adversity, feel their sadness at their failures and help them give it all to God for his healing; together, both of you will gradually appreciate more deeply how God has used them, their gifts and skills for the extension of his Kingdom and how he can use them in the future. Some people, like Maggie, will need special support – if they will accept it; but at least her inaccuracies need challenging and other people should refuse to collude with her prayer requests. It is sad if a situation gets to the stage when a person has to be asked to resign their church position because of the trouble they are causing.

Helping older people to cope with the less pleasant sides of their natures is no different from coping with this aspect of ourselves or with people of other ages, and there are many books available to help both counsellor and counselled.[1]

One thing which must be avoided is allowing others in the church or community to blame any bad behaviour on the fact that a person is old. Maggie has not changed because she has retired. It has just become more obvious, but that character trait has been there for years and gone unchallenged!

41

CHAPTER 4

The Contribution of Older People to the Church

In this chapter I want to encourage both individuals and the local church or fellowship to develop the gifts and experience that older people, including those who are physically or mentally frail, have to give to building up the whole church of Christ which is his body, recognising that they, not least because they have lived longer, have much to contribute.

However, as I highlighted in Chapter 1, society does not expect older people to have things to give and as a result many, many older people do not recognise that they have gifts to share. It requires the whole church fellowship to be on the alert and to think in new ways about who might meet a particular need. For instance, who in your church is involved in preparing young people for marriage? My suspicion is that in hardly any instance will it involve a couple over the age of sixty-five. Yet there is many an unmarried clergyman who considers himself quite capable in the area of marriage preparation. Why not a couple who have come to a deep, loving relationship through the inevitable struggles that every marriage faces at times? Older married couples, who did not have modern birth control methods like the pill available when they were young, learned far wider and deeper ways of expressing love than are mentioned today. Many of today's younger couples could save themselves and each other a lot of heartache and grow in true love through getting to know and learning from older, happily married couples. This area of ministry was brought home to me through a small brethren fellowship where an older married man called Alfred (who was not even in leadership) started taking the initiative in discussing with young men about to be married how to love and cherish their wives. The ministry soon grew, and his wife May became involved in it with him. Because of their initial openness, couples felt safe in going back and talking through further problems as they arose; a much better solution than leaving the talking until problems become so intractable that even professional marriage guidance counsellors have little help to offer.

However it is not always easy to identify what gifts an older person has; they may have lain dormant for years and the person may be reluctant to be singled out for special attention. One way could be to use one of the 'discover your gifts' charts.[1] There are many available, although it requires thought and imagination to see how they can be adapted to meet the needs of each local church. For example although Alfred and May might have realised by this method that their gift was a concern for others, it would still have required prayer and imagination to see the possibility of marriage work.

There are two ways in which 'gifts exercises' can be used. One involves the whole church. Each person can then complete a questionnaire alone or, more helpfully, have it completed by someone else as well; the two people can then compare their answers, after which they discuss how the gifts that each has might be used to build up the local church. (This method sometimes needs careful

43

handling, as through it people may realise that they are doing jobs for which they are not gifted. In more than one instance a churchwarden has discovered, what everyone else already knew but didn't have the courage to say, that leadership skills were near the bottom of his list! The problem then, of course, is helping the person to see they are doing the job for the wrong reason, probably because of a thirst for power, and then getting them to resign and develop the gift they really have.)

Another way of using these exercises is with people new to the church who have experienced a big change in their life, such as having recently got married, or retired from work, or had a stroke. Alongside the use of these exercises it is helpful to have another questionnaire listing all the jobs that need doing in the church. Be imaginative in the list. With older people, also use the list of activities in Appendix B. Because they have more time, they will be able to use their gifts for other Christian organisations as well.

Older people who are still active ought not to be treated any differently from anyone else in the congregation, and should be found undertaking all the voluntary work done by people of other ages. Is that what happens in your church? Probably not. For example, many young people's organisations ban from leadership those who are over sixty or sixty-five. Age prejudice again!

But older people's gifts with younger people can be used in other ways when they are barred by organisational rules. They may become surrogate grandparents – a marvellous way of introducing children to the joy of sharing with older people. A sympathetic older person can provide a listening ear and a retreat for young people who are at odds with their parents and having the inevitable adolescent problems. (Older people don't forget their teenage years any more or less than the rest of us!) They can teach skills, and test youngsters for their badges when there are uniformed organisations. Why use already over-worked and over-pressurised younger people when people with more time are available? One church has very successfully run joint holidays for youth club members and retired people. It's usually the youngsters that get bothered about the antics of the older people – not the other way round!

Several churches that I know depend on older people to send magazines to ex-members and to correspond regularly with younger members away at college or university. These, and writing to missionaries, are excellent jobs for those who have to spend a lot of time at home, or who are housebound. Those who are long-time members of a local church can share the history of the church with newcomers and younger people – giving a sense of community, and perhaps also helping them to appreciate why some older people may be less than enthusiastic about particular proposed changes! It also gives the opportunity for building up relationships which can lead to different points of view, when they arise, being handled positively. Older people can also share their history of the neighbourhood or community with youngsters. Living history does not have to be undertaken in stately homes or in pageants – it can be rooted in the life and experience of local people. With the frequent break-up of families, older men have much to give to even very young children. They are free during the day and can therefore be involved in pram clubs and play groups. Mending, making toys and story telling are obvious practical ways of helping. They may also help older youngsters mend their cars during holidays.

Door to door visitation and evangelism offer other possibilities for those with suitable gifts. It is surprising the number of people who are at home during the day (mothers of young children, night and shift workers, retired people), and many have more time to talk. Older people knocking at the door are also often less threatening.

Marriage preparation has already been mentioned. Older people have much to share in the whole area of pastoral care and ministry. Spiritual and psychological problems do not change – they were the same in Jesus' day (although superficially they may seem different). Paul's wise direction that older women should guide the younger women in the care of their children and households has been sadly neglected – only to be replaced in modern times by the need for 'professionals' whose advice generally has no distinct Christian perspective and is easily unthinkingly followed by non-Christians and Christians alike.

In general, theological colleges do not prepare their students to provide spiritual direction and there appears to be a great craving amongst many people for true spiritual guidance. Older people need to be encouraged to make up for this neglect. Sometimes I have asked groups of people who has most influenced their prayer life. Many, of course, say their own families, but it is interesting, as one quizzes them further, how many realise that an elderly person has played a decisive role in their spiritual growth. There is much room for encouraging this gift today, in churches of all denominations and none.

So many churches and individuals assume that prayer is the main gift that older people have to give. This is undoubtedly true, but it can sometimes be used as a way of justifying the marginalisation of older folk. When older people are asked to pray for something, how often are they asked about the answers they feel that God is giving? Some people suggest that prayer without action is of little use – what opportunities are people given to take action on the prayers they are asked to pray? What feedback do they receive? Paul shows us the close connection between prayer and thanksgiving in the Christian life – how many opportunities for thanksgiving are given to those who are asked to pray? Prayer without thanksgiving and praise leads to spiritual depression. There is a mutual responsibility to ensure that that does not happen.

Sometimes, in religious as well as secular settings, the suggestion is made that old people should provide the pastoral care of other old people. Sometimes this can be helpful, but often it is not. Even where the teaching ministry of the church is vested in certain people like the priest, minister or elders, other suitably gifted members could still be given the opportunity of running short courses on particular themes, or Bible studies, or meetings for those exploring the Christian faith. And why not hold some of these meetings in the homes of housebound members? If the cost of heating or refreshments is a problem, tactful ways of reimbursement can easily be found.

The gifts that older people have to offer the church do not vary from those that people of other ages have to offer.

What is the position in your church? To check out the situation you could list all the different voluntary jobs normally carried out. Then put down the approximate age of each person involved in each activity. Does it show age discrimination? (Or for that matter a strong class, sexual, or racial bias? But in saying that I am not suggesting that every individual activity in the church should reflect the congregational balance in every way, as that just quenches the Spirit).

If there is an imbalance, perhaps as a church you need to turn to God in prayer and work out once again what spiritual and natural gifts God has given each person and how he wants them used. An exercise of this kind will also help in identifying people who have ministries which will be of specific help to older people.

CHAPTER 5

The Churches' Care of Older People

There is a whole range of things that churches can do to support older people. The possibilities may seem overwhelming so I want to stress that the things mentioned here are just ideas, of which only one or two may be relevant to any particular church fellowship. And always the first priority is to be centred on God. Where God is Lord, he can be trusted to lead to the tasks that he wants done. 'Unless the Lord builds the house, those who build it labour in vain', is as true of building up a work with older people as it was of building the first Temple!

God may not be asking you at this stage to provide anything more specific than to enable older people to be equal with other age groups; or he may be asking you to provide a service that crosses the age range, but which will be used largely by older people. So please read this chapter prayerfully, discount ideas that don't seem relevant, identify one or two might build on what you are already doing, or use skills which are available in the church without other work suffering.

There are two dangers to be avoided: 1) to get on a bandwagon and then to leave it once the difficulties or boredom set in. When a church feels called by God to meet a need, the commitment must continue. Expectations have been raised and there is a duty to fulfil them to the best of one's ability. 2) Singling out a particular group increases the risk of them being stereotyped or even stigmatised. This has been an underlying tension for me in writing this book because I do not want older people to be patronised as some other groups are. Older people cannot be lumped together, neither are there blanket solutions to their needs. Their individuality has grown over the years. What they have a right to expect, and we have a responsibility to give, is the same level of compassion that Jesus gives. They have the same responsibility to respect and give the same level of compassion to others. We are all equal – but different – within the church of God. We have therefore the responsibility to enable older people to enter naturally into the whole life and worship of God within the local church. Where they have special needs, these must be met with a quiet dignity.

Church Buildings and Services

No one should be unable to enter into the public worship of God. Does your church provide access for disabled or wheelchair-bound people? The provision of a permanent ramp may be too expensive or structurally impossible, but have portable ramps or a stair lift been considered? Sometimes even the rehanging of doors or the provision of rails alongside steps aid the confidence of those who are not steady on their feet. Are the steps clearly indicated by bold edges? The social services department's occupational therapists should be able to give advice and they are usually only too willing to do so with regard to problems affecting disabled people.[1]

Can people hear service leaders and preachers easily? If a microphone is used, or there is an amplification system, it is cheap and easy to add an 'induction loop' for the hard of hearing who use aids. The 'loop system' can even be added to the portable systems so many churches use for open air work. It can also be used in halls and ancillary buildings as well.[2]

Are there hymn boards, so that even if people miss the announcement they can find their place easily?

Some illnesses require drug treatments which mean that people need to go to the toilet frequently. Are toilets easily accessible? Even if structural and/or financial difficulties prevent proper toilet facilities being installed, most churches have some room or area which could be converted to take caravan-type portable toilets.

Churches are increasingly replacing pews with more flexible forms of seating. Back problems affect many people – not just those who are elderly – and thought needs to be given to what will be most suitable. Where possible it is helpful to have some chairs with arms – it is much easier to get up from them, and church services demand an awful lot of getting up and sitting down (many people feel conspicuous if they remain seated all the time). When buying, ask the advice of those who struggle as to which will be the most suitable.

Good lighting – but without glare – is essential, as is the use of non-slip wax on floors, and also of carpets which are tacked down.

It is possible to buy most hymn books and Bibles in a large print format so always try to have some available (and when replacing books don't buy ones that have no large print editions!); home-produced chorus sheets can be magnified on the photocopier for those who need them; check that hymns or choruses put on acetates for use on overhead projectors

51

are written in black felt tip pen in good size lettering. I find ¼-inch small case is clearest (NB: typed acetates are not easy to read from a distance). The aim of doing all this should be to enable everyone, irrespective of age, to be able to enter into the worship of God without hassle, and for no one to feel conspicuous in any way. Anything done for handicapped or elderly people will normally be appreciated by the able-bodied anyway.

Increasingly, churches are serving tea and/or coffee after services. It is helpful to have a few firmer, stronger plastic holders for use by those with a poor hand grip. They will often feel less embarrassed, too, if their cups are not filled too full. Where china is used, check out with individuals what they find most suitable and certainly keep one or two clean atractive mugs for handicapped people who might suddenly turn up.

Transport

Organising lifts to church is a big area of need in many churches – if only because any systematic house visitation programme will result in people needing lifts. It is always risky just to hope that lifts will be offered as necessary. Jane, parts of whose story I shared in Chapter 2, is only able to go to church in the evening if she is sure of a lift home. She told me:

> Some time ago I was at a church meeting and the minister said, 'You're not to walk home', but he didn't say who was going to take me. Almost everyone had gone and the minister still hadn't done anything so I asked someone. They said no, they couldn't. I'll never ask anyone

again. It is so embarrassing. Then one day someone said, 'If you'll wait whilst I clear up, I'll take you home,' and they've done it ever since.

It is often easier if there is one person who acts as the co-ordinator. Not everyone with a car can offer lifts every week, and lifts also need to be arranged for other church activities, both regular and occasional. The co-ordinator does not necessarily need to have a car themselves – in fact this is a very suitable job for a person who is handicapped – but they do need to be gifted administratively, and to be easily contactable by telephone. As with all jobs, out-of-pocket expenses should be reimbursed – telephone costs add up very quickly. These days it is not only frail people who can benefit from lifts; buses are unreliable, and in country areas people can have to travel several miles on some Sundays in order to attend service. A transport scheme can therefore help a far wider group of the congregation.

The Church and Housebound People

Many individuals and church groups find that they can quite easily begin supporting their older people by 'just visiting'. But those new to it are often worried about what to say and how to cope if the older person is slow to respond. It might be helpful to bear in mind some practical points here.

The first thing is that older people may have a different perspective on time. How they view it will be very individual depending on how much time they have to spend on chores, how much time they spend alone and their attitude to life. It is likely that most people will speak and think more slowly. It is NOT a sign of senile dementia – it is much more likely to be a sign that they are in touch with God's natural rhythm of time. They can help us all resist the temptation to conform to the world's rat race.

They will also have a different perspective on the number of visitors they have. Having one visitor for ten minutes each day when confined to the house and then spending the other 1430 minutes alone isn't going to have much significance!

If someone lives alone they are unlikely to be aware of any loss of hearing. Some types of hearing loss mean that people only hear parts of words or the sounds are distorted. This can lead to them giving totally wrong responses. They do not suffer from senile dementia. They may well be able to hear the rest of what is said without using a raised voice so they will quite rightly say that they aren't deaf. They will need special hospital examination (out-patients) in order to diagnose the problem.

Where a person is hard of hearing or wears a deaf aid they will find it easier to cope if the light is falling on your face so they can lip read as well. Usually, however, shouting doesn't help so speak distinctly. If they don't understand what you're saying, rephrase it.

Try and let them do things for you. If they can make cakes, all be it with a struggle, and want to for your visit, accept graciously. No doubt you will want to continue to offer hospitality to visitors when you grow older and it is an important way of giving thanks to someone who is helping us. Mrs Hegarty (page 84) describes vividly the importance of this tradition to her.

Knowing when to end a visit can be difficult. Obviously if the person is beginning to tire you should leave but sometimes you can have the opposite problem and find it difficult to get away! Having another appointment, eg picking children up from school can be useful but you need to be sensitive because it is easy to come across as being patronising.

The church can also help sick and housebound people to feel part of the congregation by taping services which can be lent to them. This is easy to do once there is a microphone system, as even a cheap tape recorder can be plugged straight into that. If a visitor can stay and listen to the service with the housebound person, this gives added meaning and a focus for discussion, but even when that does not happen, dropping a tape in gives a reason for a visit – and this often helps break the ice for someone new to visiting. For the few who cannot get out to services at all, receiving tapes regularly helps them to feel they still belong. Where there is a prayer letter or church newsletter/ magazine this can be delivered at the same time. (The system should not be exclusively for those who are elderly or frail – many mums with tiny babies or toddlers go through a phase when attending church is either impossible because of the baby's routine or else they can't concentrate because their minds are disturbed by little Johnny's restlessness. They, too, can benefit from listening at home.)

The BBC Radio 4 mid-morning weekday service has a very large audience. A local church can use this as a focus of prayer amongst those who are home during the day, particularly those who are frail. One church I knew encouraged regular listening, and then suggested that church members should go on to pray from the church's daily prayer list, and also for each other. God gave a marvellous sense of unity as people shared together, albeit at a distance from one another. Perhaps this is the modern equivalent of the custom by which people in earlier generations prayed whenever they heard the church bell ring, knowing that they were part of the worshipping community even when separated by sickness or work. The mid-morning 'meeting' can include others who are at home during the day. It is a valuable way of embracing people who, for some reason, are becoming forgetful. They can still feel involved and yet if they forget it does not cause problems for anyone.

Special Services

It may be right occasionally to focus for a day on older people – in the same way as there are harvest or children's festivals in some churches.

One church I know set aside a weekend and called it 'Celebrating Age'. They set up an exhibition in the church covering the achievements of older people in the community and provided information about different aspects of successful ageing. The church was open throughout the weekend for people to look round. On the Sunday there was a special service planned and led by older members, and the preacher was an ex-minster, now retired. It is a simple idea and could be copied quite easily by many churches and fellowships.

Evangelism

In Chapter 2 I briefly mentioned sharing the gospel with older people. Churches involved in outreach work will discover many older people, and members directly involved will benefit from knowing how to approach them. Visitors need to listen carefully, to pick up the older person's concerns and to respond to them.

Josie came to faith through a London City missioner who knocked on her door as she was worrying about how to get to hospital for her out-patient's appointment the following week. He arranged help through the hospital transport service, went back afterwards to find out how she had got on and then visited again when she went in for the operation, and left some literature with her. At her request he read from the Gideon's Bible in her locker. After she came out he continued to visit, and soon she started attending the local mission hall and is now a committed member.

Door-to-door work also brings the church into contact with those who for one reason or another have drifted away. They can be quite nervous of becoming recommitted, and of the reception they will get if they return. Time is of the essence but sometimes door-to-door evangelists do not realise this and are concerned to cover as big an area as quickly as possible. This is where some older people in the team, who have more time to spare, can help. The team might, too, use one or two of the housebound church members as 'prayer shadows' whilst they are out, making sure they get a 'report back' afterwards for their encouragement.

When door-knocking, one usually finds some sick people. I am always surprised (although I shouldn't be) at how many welcome prayer. It needs to be offered in such a way that it is easy for the person to say 'no' but it can, over several visits, lead the way to talking more deeply about Jesus as Lord and Saviour.

As far as possible, older enquirers and converts should be treated in the same way as younger people – not least because it helps everyone to experience the equality and mutuality that the church is ideally practising. But like other converts they will benefit from one-to-one nurturing as well as the general group meetings, and then it is probably right for them to be linked with someone of similar age.

Baptism, Confirmation and Communion

In some denominations, decisions about how an elderly convert is received into membership are made by senior leaders, but in many churches the decision is made locally. One point to bear in mind is that the Bible seems to assume that everyone is to be received and that no exceptions should occur because of age. However, difficulties do arise if a church practises baptism by immersion; or a person is too frail to come to church for confirmation; or is unable to be present at public celebrations of the Lord's Supper.

Where a church generally baptises by immersion, or at a church service, thought needs to be given to the implications for refusing baptism if a person is too frail either mentally or physically. Is the amount of water important? Does baptism have to take place in a certain building? Is it important to fulfil the Lord's injunction in spite of *all* obstacles? What account should be taken of the person's own feelings and preferences? Will previous contact with another denomination affect the decision? Is membership and reception possible without baptism? Is there any place for communion at home? If so, can the person be alone or should it be with other church members? There are no simple answers to these questions but they cannot be ignored if presenting the Gospel to people of all ages is taken seriously. It will not help a 'young' older Christian if they suddenly find themselves at the centre of a controversy, or if logical explanations are not forthcoming when 'full' membership is denied them.

Anointing and Praying for the Sick

In some churches this practice has no place, but in others there is response to the injunction of James 5.14 – 'Is any among you sick? Let him call for the elders of the church and let them pray over him, anointing him with oil in the name of the Lord.' How it is worked out varies enormously from local church to local church. It is particularly important to explain it carefully to the person concerned. Some of today's older folk may associate it with the Roman Catholic and Anglo-Catholic rite of some years ago, when anointing was primarily seen as the preparation for imminent death. If it is practised with the expectation of healing, then the leaders must ensure that the elderly person is quite clear on the purpose of the prayer and the anointing. Many older people may be very diffident about asking for prayer for health. Obviously they should not feel pressurised, but they need encouragement to talk about it. When a person is very frail, it is generally much better undertaken quietly with just three or four people at most present, although other church members may be praying at home or in church.

Sensitivity will be needed about the length of the service, and whether it should include communion. This will vary according to local church practice; but it is important not to get into a set routine which hinders people from feeling that they are special, and which prevents the Holy Spirit from teaching new ways of ministry. It is the way in which Jesus responded in a different way to every individual's cry for help, and the power and the love that his Spirit gives, that should characterise our ministry in his name. Prayer for healing in old age is not essentially different from prayer for health at other ages but the natural ageing process must be taken into account and this is particularly important in ministry with very frail people.

Use of Church Buildings

Another possible area of development is to use church premises for group activities for older people. A church may feel that it can support a lunch club or day centre for older people once a week. On the other hand it may be more sensible to offer the facilities to a secular organisation to use, with perhaps one or two church members acting as helpers. (Your local Citizens Advice Bureau will be able to tell you the most sensible people to discuss your proposals with.) Which option you prefer will depend on how your church views its mission to older people in its community.

There is a desperate need in many places for facilities and people to run small groups for people with Alzheimer's disease (also known as senile dementia). People with that disease are very sensitive to atmosphere, and the peace and serenity of many church facilities can provide an environment which helps them keep in touch with themselves and other people. If you are willing to consider this service you will find people from the local community psychiatric service, or the specialist psychiatrist in the diseases of old age, only too willing to talk and help you to explore the possibilities.

Over recent years there have been many exciting developments involving a new church integrated with the provision of housing for older people as well as families. Generally it is helpful to do this in partnership with specialist housing associations. For example, the Shaftesbury Society has extensive experience in the provision of sheltered housing for elderly or physically handicapped people. It is also worth contacting the Centre on the Environment for the Handicapped who have produced a lot of architectural advice on the needs of handicapped people and maintain a list of architects who have a special interest in this area of work.

Co-ordinating Care

Throughout this book I stress the importance of meeting the needs of elderly people on an individual basis, so that anyone interested in forming links with older people can do so irrespective of their church's policy.

However where there are a number of older people in the church, or a developing ministry to older people in the area, then it will probably benefit from some co-ordination. This ensures that people don't get missed or 'drop through the net'. Co-ordination also means that church members who are feeling particularly pressured or bogged down by a person's problems have someone else to talk with, and hopefully others who might help in sharing the burden. For example, Chapter 6 is concerned with the time-consuming decisions faced by someone thinking about entering an old people's home. Where several people work together, the commitment involved becomes much more manageable. Co-ordination can also ensure that housebound or frail people do not miss out on special church events, that they get magazines or literature regularly, and that if someone has to give up visiting, someone else in the church can be asked to take their place.

The scheme does not have to be exclusively for frail people. In one church the co-ordinator is also responsible for seeing that people who have drifted from regular attendance at church for one reason or another are followed up, and that the families of mentally handicapped and disturbed youngsters are also cared for.

I have found that people permanently admitted to hospital or a home too easily get forgotten. Sometimes visits continue for a while, but then the key visitor withdraws or moves and no one else takes over. Where there is a co-ordinator this is much less likely to happen as someone else can take their place.

It is also useful to have one person (either the same co-ordinator or someone else) who is responsible for informing hospital chaplains about hospital admissions even when it is only for a few days. Most Christians find it comforting to have prayer just before an operation and it is not always possible for church or fellowship leaders to visit at the critical time.

Another co-ordinating role is to ensure that older people are aware of secular services that are available when they need them. It is surprising and

sad how often churches struggle on helping an individual because they are unaware of what is available from other statutory and voluntary agencies.
This can particularly apply when people come out
of hospital. Church care during the early days can
be invaluable, as most people relapse at least a
little after discharge. However, if they do not pick
up quickly, a variety of services are available.
Churches need to make sure that people tap into
them. It is easy for a person's response to the doctor's question to be 'I'm all right, So-and-so is
getting a meal for me.' The doctor then thinks they
are being cared for adequately, when the service is
in fact being provided at great inconvenience.

The co-ordinator's role may also include watching that visitors do not take on too much, or get
into situations that are beyond their capacity to
cope with.

Those with a commitment to caring will also
benefit from meeting together occasionally, and
sometimes hearing a speaker on some topic of relevance to their concerns. A co-ordinator can organise this. They should also know where to get
information on coping with various problems; act
as a resource to others in the church; and pass on
information about meetings held by other organisations which might be of interest.

The church may choose to divide the roles so that
no one person has too much to do. In churches that
have care groups, it should be possible for older
people, even when housebound, to be part of these.

Confidentiality

Gossip is a major problem in many churches, and
meetings of any kind can be a hotbed for it. Older

people are not going to open up on their deeper concerns if they think they are going to be talked about. Boundaries of confidentiality therefore need to be understood and explicitly stated. This includes deciding what and when information is passed on to ministers, elders and other church leaders. A useful principle is that only the person who has the problem has the right to share it or give their agreement to it being shared with others. Those receiving information, or giving support, have no right to share it with anyone without the knowledge and agreement of the person concerned. On rare occasions when information has to be shared without a person's agreement, they must be told in advance that this is going to happen. Where there is a co-ordinator it may be generally accepted that visitors discuss difficulties with them. But make sure that all those being visited are aware that this happens. Gossips do not make suitable visitors. Where a church sets a high standard of confidentiality, people are paradoxically much more willing to be open because they are able to trust each other much more deeply.

Some churches have a system of elders or overseers, each of whom is responsible for a certain number of members. Even then it may be more sensible to have others to be responsible for specific areas of need, to whom elders and overseers can go for more detailed advice.

However, whilst the co-ordinating and visiting roles can be undertaken by lay people, it is essential that there is very close liaison between visitors and the church minister or leaders so that their view of what is happening in the church does not become distorted and they lose touch with the less articulate and forceful members of the church.

This provides a marvellous opportunity, if it is done sensitively, for the church to go to people – so often we wait for people to come to the church. There are not many places in the country where the local church could not develop a ministry of this sort. Independent churches do not have parish boundary problems, and Anglican and Roman Catholic churches, even if they have no homes in their parishes, can always make contact with hospital chaplains about helping at hospital services. (Non-conformist and independent churches can contact the non-conformist hospital chaplain.)

Getting Services Going

Whether a service can be held in a residential home or sheltered housing unit depends on the attitude of the person in charge, and it is important to take time to build up a relationship with them. They will see the offer from the wider perspective of the needs of residents and tenants, and may want you to get involved in providing other help, such as outings or entertainment, and you must decide whether this is feasible. They will be concerned that people do not feel hi-jacked into attending something against their will – this particularly applies if there is only one sitting room which everyone has to share. If there are a number of possible sheltered housing schemes or homes (but during the rest of this chapter I will just use the term 'home') in your area, you may decide to visit several to see which is likely to be most welcoming – this is particularly important if it is your first experience of providing this type of ministry. Another good way is to approach the person in charge of a home in which you already have a member resident, or where a church member works.

In some places there will be many homes in a small area. Rather than try to cover the lot it is much better to begin by focusing on one, and then, once that is working smoothly, start a service in another home and so gradually expand. Starting something new takes more time and energy than is often realised and it is a process which cannot be hurried.

Forming the Team

Informal services are a very good way for church members to develop their gifts, but services must nevertheless be honouring to God and of a high standard. They are not places to send people who have no gift and just want a public platform! This particularly applies to those who provide the talk – they must be able to speak clearly, simply, briefly and deeply through identification with the residents' or tenants' real needs, and be able to encourage them in their faith.

It is helpful to have at least one good musician – preferably with a portable instrument – in each team to give a strong lead, and do check out any pianos as they often tend to be out of tune! It is worth remembering that people with poor memories or with speech problems usually find singing easier than speaking. Most people enjoy singing, so during a service of twenty to thirty minutes have several hymns and choruses, concentrating initially on the ones people know. Later, new ones can gradually be introduced – particularly those which are short and have catchy tunes. Copyright on hymns generally ceases fifty years after the death of the writer so many hymns can be copied quite freely. Increasingly the more recent hymns and choruses are covered by a cheap licensing agreement which most churches would find useful.[3]

It is important for the team to have a co-ordinator so that everyone follows a similar theme, and where possible those taking any lead should get together beforehand to check that it all meshes together.

The co-ordinator also needs to confirm arrangements with the home – for instance, if the service is on the first Sunday of the month the leader needs to ring early the previous week to check that all is well. Sometimes, especially if it is in a group of sheltered housing flats, a poster needs to be put up on the notice board. Where possible it is also helpful to do this in homes.

Ideally the team should have at least half a dozen members, so that people are available to help residents find their places, give a lead to the singing and create a friendly atmosphere. That number also allows for time to be spent with every resident either before or after the service. You will be amazed how many have a faith, although it may have remained dormant for years, and regular personal contact can allow it to flower again. And you will find after a while that at least some people will welcome a lift to church services, either when there is something special, or on a more regular basis.

Probably you will find that membership of the team varies from time to time, but always try to make sure that at least half are well known in the home. When things go well and church members enjoy going, a team usually likes to stay together; but where the going is heavy or there are a lot of mentally frail people, swopping around helps to keep people enthusiastic.

Keeping Services Going

It is often easier to start something than it is to keep it going afterwards, and services in old people's homes and sheltered housing flats are no different. If they are beginning to seem dull and lifeless, try to work out the reason why. Are the team losing enthusiasm? If so, then it may be time for them to have a social get-together or go out for an evening or to share their joys and struggles about the home. Others will feel it right to pray and fast.

Do residents seem restless? It may be because they are feeling unsure of what is expected of them, or be new, or have some other reason. It can be good then for a team member to sit on the floor beside them, just giving a reassuring touch from time to time, sharing a hymn sheet or communicating acceptance in some way. Occasionally people are at the service when they do not want to be, and then it is a good idea to spend special time with them afterwards, tactfully trying to discover the reason why and, if necessary, ensuring that they are not made to stay another time.

Sometimes services become dull through lack of variety or because there is too much talking from the front. Getting residents to participate by choosing hymns helps, and if it tends to be dominated by one or two people then ask individuals afterwards which are their favourite hymns and use them the next time, explaining who has chosen them. It might be possible to show a *short* religious video from time to time (but remember it is very like the TV that dominates so many homes) and then have a discussion afterwards or draw out one or two points. Children are always popular, and perhaps members of the Sunday school or youth club could occasionally do part of something they have done in church.

If you have the time and resources there is a lot of value in visiting the home during the week, taking residents on an occasional outing or bringing them to a church function. To do that you will need suitable transport – either a minibus, probably with a tail lift facility, or more likely several cars. Not everyone needs to be included every time, but make sure everyone has the chance before you start asking people for the second time.

People probably will not want to go far, but those who do not get out often, enjoy seeing once again the places they have known in the past. Perhaps a neighbouring church with adequate toilet facilities would lay on tea and some other church members could join in at that point.

Activities like this allow people the chance to share their anxieties or personal struggles. They allow church members to get to know older or frail people and above all allow older people to be strengthened and challenged to grow in their knowledge and love of God. Services in old people's homes are a marvellous opportunity to bring God close to people at a time in life when their physical and emotional environment can be very limited. Sadly, the number of fellowships willing to undertake this ministry are few.

One Church's Experience of Developing Services in Old People's Homes

Some work with older people can grow naturally out of the interest and enthusiasm of one or two people. It can grow, too, through an increasing number of older folk in the church. But it can also come as a planned change.

An enthusiastic Baptist layman felt that as their church was big, gifted and in an area filled with residential and nursing homes, they should be making contact with residents in some of them, and providing for their spiritual needs. He discussed his ideas with his pastor and elders, who were happy for him to explore the possibility further, particularly as the church was about to have a theological student with them for a year. The proviso was that whatever developed must provide opportunities for sharing the gospel. He got three other committed people, and together they set a time scale and worked out a strategy. During the next month they visited a number of homes and asked the people in charge how best they could serve the residents. They were fortunate in meeting the owner of several homes who invited them to take services in the homes he owned. Not all the officers in charge were so keen! Eventually the steering group identified a dozen homes who would welcome regular church visits.

Alongside this they met to think and pray about which homes to start in (in their minds they'd planned on twelve homes in twelve months) and how they could recruit a team. As the church has about 500 members, it was not possible to know everyone who might be interested in joining a team, who had the necessary gifts, or who had gifts which could be developed. They were also anxious to avoid any sense of rivalry with existing activities, and were determined that people would come first. They had learned from previous experience that blanket appeals did not get sufficient response. In the congregation they had a young man who was good at making audio tapes. They enlisted his help in making a tape/slide presentation of the project.

Feeling confident that the plans were reasonably concrete so that they could follow up and use offers of help speedily (a crucial factor in maintaining enthusiasm), they arranged to get the leaders of all the church activities together for a social evening at which they shared their ideas, gave the tape/slide presentation and answered questions. They then asked leaders to think about which members of their groups might be interested initially in sharing in a 'one off' service with no further commitment attached. The leaders could either approach people themselves or let the steering group have names of people to follow up. These activity leaders were also asked to get their groups to pray regularly for the project. The steering group then contacted everyone who had said they wanted to contribute.

Within a month there had been 'experimental services' in three homes, and everyone involved then met to review how they had gone and to decide how they should proceed. Most people had enjoyed themselves so much that they wanted to continue on a regular basis. However, the steering group soon discovered that they had been very over-ambitious in aiming at twelve homes in twelve months, and at the end of the first year had monthly services in four, and that increased to six during the next year.

The original enthusiast did not become the coordinator of the project; instead someone who was gifted administratively took on the role. He found it was important to get everyone together every few months to share what had been happening. Where there was real participation from the residents he found that the service team wanted to stick together. However at one home – Springfield – where all the residents have senile dementia and where it is difficult to get involvement, the team has been much less stable. As a result the coordinator asks members of other service teams to go to Springfield occasionally, and ensures that members of the Springfield team get the opportunity to go to other homes from time to time as well; unless they want to stay, team members only go there for a year. In this way continuity is provided and yet people do not get too bogged down.

Conclusion

These are just some of a whole variety of ways in which a church's concern for older people can be developed. The way God works this out will be very different for every church, but one thing is essential, and that is that older people are enabled to feel as important a part of the church as the children, young people or families. When any local church focuses primarily on one particular group (unless it is a church within a self-contained community, such as a church on a university campus), then prejudice against other groups becomes almost impossible to avoid. It is the stress on young people, so often referred to as the church of tomorrow, that has led many older people to practise their faith outside the confines of the institutional Church. We have the challenge of deepening our faith through work with them.

CHAPTER 6

Moving Home

The next three chapters concentrate on issues that concern individual older people; the ways in which as individuals, irrespective of local church policy and attitudes, they can be enabled to continue to grow in the knowledge and love of God and, to adapt a quotation from the Anglican Baptism Service prayer, continue to 'fight valiantly under the banner of Christ against sin, the world and the devil, and to continue God's faithful soldiers and servants to the end of their lives'.

Many older people move home at retirement or when they become frail. For most people, of any age, moving is an upheaval and physically exhausting. There is also sadness (even when it involves an exciting new phase to life, like marriage) as memories of a particular home come flooding back. Rachel, whose story I shared in Chapter 1, and who had to move against her will, still looks back nostalgically to her previous home. Being forced to move, an experience many of today's older people have known, either through the war or through various governments' housing policies of the '60s and '70s, makes adjustment to the new circumstances much more difficult. This needs to be borne in mind when older people face a change. Perhaps they can no longer manage stairs, have an outside toilet, or lack a bathroom, find the buses to the nearest shopping centre are withdrawn, or that they can no longer afford to run a car. Sometimes, at retirement, people are forced to move because the house is too big or expensive to maintain or they need capital to increase their weekly income.

Freqently moves are suggested or explored without thinking through all the options. For example, where neglected repairs are a problem it is sometimes possible to get grants. Help may be available with major repairs like a new roof, installation of an indoor bathroom and toilet, or the conversion of a house into flats. In some circumstances even private tenants can apply.

For home owners, banks, building societies and local authorities provide loans and/or mortgage annuity option schemes. Age Concern England publishes books and continuously updated fact sheets on them and so it is best to get the information as the need arises.[1] New schemes are being introduced all the time. However, the upheaval caused by major building works should not be underestimated, and a move to somewhere more suitable may often be more sensible. In that case the person may welcome help in thinking through what type of accommodation they want – and what are the chances of their getting it. Do they want to move nearer relatives? (But what would happen if those relatives themselves were to move or die?) Would they like to live in a retirement village, with a small number of other retired people, or do they prefer being primarily among younger people? Do they want to stay in the same neighbourhood, go to the same church, live with people of a similar background? Do they need a flat without steps or stairs? Do they want somewhere quiet? Do they need easy access to public transport? Which do they prefer – independent housing or somewhere with a warden on call? If the latter, have they considered one of the alarm schemes being developed by a range of companies using the telephone as the means of getting emergency help? (Age Concern can provide information about these.)

Unless public sector housing is involved it is unlikely that professionals will be advising the elderly person so it is very important that older people are alerted to the options available.

Obviously people who own their own homes have the widest choice. If they are thinking of buying a flat in a private, sheltered housing scheme, then they need to take very careful legal advice. What are the service charges, and are these likely to increase as people in the scheme become frailer? Are there any clauses in the agreements which suggest people must leave if they become frail? What are the arrangements for having visitors – particularly for a few days? Who makes the choice when a new warden is needed? What are his or her duties? Who makes sure he or she carries them out properly? What are the conditions regarding the sale of the flat if they leave the scheme?

Some of these questions can occur if the person is thinking of moving into a housing association scheme or into an almshouse. Most voluntary organisations will not take people with a lot of capital and some only take people living in the same locality or with specific church connections, but it is sometimes possible to move to this type of accommodation if the person has relatives in the neighbourhood. Other housing associations and almshouses are for people who worked in specific trades or professions; for example the Gardeners' Benevolent Fund only accept people who were employed as gardeners during their working lives. Information about all these options can be quite difficult to track down but your local Citizens Advice Bureau and the National Federation of Housing

Associations (see Appendix D for address) should be able to give you some clues.

Helping With the Move Itself

It is easy to underestimate the amount of thought and energy needed in coping with practical tasks associated with a move and most people, whatever their age, welcome help with them. If a group of people from the church can help, the burden will be eased. It is a delicate balance to provide enough support and yet to avoid the person feeling that others are taking over. It helps if just one person co-ordinates the church aid and makes sure that the older person is consulted at every stage and given as much time as possible to make each decision.

When the move involves changing churches it can be quite difficult to identify a church in the new area which will meet the person's spiritual needs (particularly if they cannot walk far and therefore have little choice). It takes a generous, warm-hearted church to be willing to provide the practical help someone needs when they do not already know them. Churches which genuinely care about newcomers will have information available about shopping facilities, doctors (especially those who have a concern for older people), local amenities, etc.

Going to Live with Relatives

If a person becomes difficult or seems 'forgetful', relatives, neighbours or concerned church friends tend to feel that he or she may no longer be able to live alone. Often when someone has been bereaved of a spouse, relatives panic and it is easy for decisions to be made without proper thought. There is also an enormous amount of pressure on other family members to provide a home or extensive care for frail relatives.

The Bible has a lot to say about respecting older people and caring for sick relatives but it is important to maintain a balanced perspective. Jesus as he was dying asked John to care for his mother – not his family, although he had both half-brothers and sisters. Many people are at some time faced with the dilemma, either in terms of pressure being put upon them to care, or later in life having to consider whether the person should live with younger relatives.

Those who care about frail people will be drawn into family situations where this will be an issue, and advice and help may be sought. It is important, if you find yourself asked for advice, that your own subjective feelings and assumptions are recognised and accepted and that you are careful not to let these influence the older person and their family. It is not easy to listen to both points of view and it is often easier if one helper supports the person concerned whilst someone else supports other family members. A wrong decision can have far-reaching implications. Here are some areas which all the parties need to discuss openly together.

1) What accommodation will the person have, and is it really suitable for their needs? 2) How are the domestic arrangements going to be organised – meals, washing and ironing, cleaning etc? 3) To what extent will they live as part of the family and to what extent independently? 4) How easy will it be for them to have personal visitors without it intruding on the rest of the family? What if guests want to

stay overnight? 5) To what extent will the lifestyles of the different generations create conflict – and how will the conflict be resolved? Do the different generations get on together now? If there will be young people around, will a frail person be able to cope with noise, late nights etc? 6) There also needs to be real honesty about how good the relationships were forty, fifty or sixty years previously. Two, three or four generations living together are frequently very happy but everyone needs to behave very maturely if it is to work out. Where relationships have been poor in the past they are not likely to change for the better, without an enormous struggle, now that one party is old and frail.

Once the individual has moved in with their family they are very unlikely ever to have a separate home of their own again, so that if it does not work out, the only likely alternative will be a residential home. They can feel rejected and powerless, while younger relatives can feel guilty and angry.

Residential Care

It is very difficult for someone to return to living independently once they have entered a residential home. This option is therefore something to be thought about very seriously. Some people are glad to give up running their own home, revel in the company of others and so enjoy communal living. But for most people it is a choice made from necessity, so it is important that all the possible options are explored carefully.

Over the next few years more social workers should become availabe to help with this process, and from April 1991 local authorities will be completely responsible for meeting the fees of people entering all types of residential homes whose own financial resources are insufficient.

When a person is finding it difficult to cope, it is helpful if they can have a thorough medical check-up to make sure that there is no treatment which could improve their health. Remember, old age itself is not a sickness, so that any incapacity will be due to a disease which will have a medical label. It is amazing how often ill health in older people is taken for granted. It is also worth asking how you can contact an occupational therapist to assess whether aids would enable the person to stay at home longer.

It is easy for younger people to go to a home and see it as attractively furnished, with a nice garden and perhaps a view, several lounges and meals provided three times a day, plus drinks, and so it is important to think a bit more deeply about the experience:

1. Imagine you are going to a home where fortunately you will have a room to yourself which you will be able to furnish as you wish. It is ten feet square, there is a wash basin, a fitted wardrobe and a window which takes up most of one wall with a radiator underneath it. Now go round your home and decide what you will take with you in the way of furniture, personal possessions and clothes.

2. Now imagine how you are going to occupy your day. You can't walk for more than about fifteen minutes (and you won't have a car or be able to drive one!) Think about always having your meals with other people – and they would not necessarily be people you would choose to mix with. You will have no choice over who

cleans your room and provides any personal attention you may need. You will have little privacy.

I suspect if you did the experiment honestly and realistically you found that you have to leave behind many things that mean a lot to you. How easy did you find it to work out how you would spend your time? Would you be so enthusiastic when it was the three hundredth day, or after three years? How about always being among people? Imagine living, eating and sleeping permanently with all other members of your church or fellowship group! It is hard working at relationships at the best of times; poor health makes it much harder.

Choosing a Suitable Home

But assuming all these alternatives have been explored, then the person still needs to think about what type of home would best be able to meet their needs. Sometimes, particularly if they cannot afford private home fees, they may have an experienced professional to discuss the possibilities with them, but if they are paying for themselves this is unlikely. *Residential homes* (which do not provide skilled nursing care) can be run by voluntary organisations, private individuals or local authorities. Information about homes in any particular locality can be obtained from the local social services offices. But finding out about voluntary homes is generally more difficult. Some only take people from particular areas, others are for people with particular trade or professional backgrounds, others will accept anyone. Quite a number are run by Christian groups – sometimes for members of a particular denomination, others for anyone with an active Christian faith, whilst still others accept anyone. A list of some of the larger Christian organisations can be found in Appendix E. Where lists of private homes over a wider area, such as a county, are needed, they can be got from a Citizens Advice Bureau in that area or the social services department head office.

There are also *private nursing homes* which provide care for very frail people who are probably incontinent and need the type of care that long-stay hospitals usually give.

The quality and atmosphere in homes varies enormously and there are good, bad and indifferent ones in every sector.

Now a word about finance. Until April 1991 people in local authority homes will pay according to their means, the local authority meeting the remainder of the cost. Those in private and voluntary-run homes with insufficient resources can get help (although there is a fees limit) through the Department of Social Security. The person will be well advised to get help from a Citizens Advice Bureau or from Care and Counsel for the Elderly, Twyman House, 16 Bonny Street, London NW1, who can also sometimes help to put people in touch with organisations that can give additional grants if the State benefit – Income Support – is insufficient.

It is essential to be sure that any particular home can provide the care the person needs before they take steps to dispose of their own home; whilst someone else can eliminate those homes that are least suitable, it is essential that the person visits possible places and makes their own choice. It helps if they can visit several homes (after all buying a house is not usually a quick decision, nor do people just look at one property), so they can make comparisons and get used to asking questions that matter. There is no reason either why they should not revisit places that seem more suitable. This is where churches can be helpful, in providing people with transport, going through issues beforehand that will need covering, helping them talk through their feelings afterwards. It is time-consuming, but it is not a task that will arise very often.

Here are some points the person may want to think over:

1. Will they have a single room, or if not, how many people will they be sharing with?
2. What choices are there about staying in their room during the day?
3. What about meals, their times, and where they have them?
4. What are the arrangements about TV programmes, lounges, smoking, making cups of tea and coffee for themselves and guests?
5. Where are visitors entertained and when?
6. What can they take to the home with them?
7. Can they have their own doctor, call him and see him alone?
8. Do they keep their own medicines or drugs?
9. What house rules are there?
10. What happens about their room or bed if they need hospital in-patient treatment?
11. Will they need to leave if they become more frail?
12. How do residents spend their time and what activities are organised?

When looking around a home, watch what is happening. Do staff seem to know and respond to residents warmly? Do staff talk to the prospective resident or direct their remarks to the person accompanying them? Do residents seem lethargic, bored or alert and happy?

After the visit, encourage the person to think through the situation. What attracted them to the home? What did they dislike? What will they find difficult to accept? Did they like the residents and staff they spoke with? Is the home easily accessible to relatives and friends who will visit (particularly those without their own transport)?

It is always a good idea for a person to pay several day visits to a potential home, and whenever possible to have at least a couple of weeks' stay. It allows them to know what they are letting themselves in for before they burn their boats.

Once a home has been chosen, some people start clearing out their homes and want the whole episode over as soon as possible. This is understandable. Good homes often have a waiting list and waiting is very stressful. They need as much support as possible and should be discouraged from hasty action. Help them share their feelings – probably sorrow, anger and pain – or be prepared at times just to stand alongside, even though you may not get any thanks! Remember, they are leaving a home which has many memories and they will have had to part with possessions they may have had for sixty, seventy or eighty years.

Standing alongside means you too will experience a lot of pain, and it can take a long time. It may therefore be helpful for two or three people to support each other and the older person concerned, so that the load is shared. It is my experience that crises never spread themselves but tend to come in one go! Pray together if you can, and with the person. Continue to involve them in other activities and interests – there is a real danger of them opting out and getting very depressed, which will only mean they will cope less and less well.

Entering the Home Permanently

Some people, on entering a residential or nursing home, will want to be involved in disposing of their home, but it is my experience that most prefer to leave it to someone else. Amongst this generation of older people, the experience of entering a home for a woman is very like retiring from work for a man. Suddenly she no longer has a whole range of decisions to make or jobs to do. How is her time to be used? She has been used to living alone; suddenly she has to get used to a new routine, new people – all with their own idiosyncracies and no choice in who helps her with any personal needs she has.

Mrs Hegarty described her experience to me:

Everyone is very kind to me and we are very well looked after. I came in just for a rest, just to see whether I would fit in. I didn't mean to come in and give up my home. But I was very happy and knew I would not mind coming back again. Of course I had mixed feelings. I can't do this, that and the other that I've done for so long. But you have to settle; I couldn't carry on. The old way's finished.

When I was at home I had lots of friends visit me. We used to have tea together – that's the worst. We can't any more. I can't get tea for them. Mrs — is very nice and we have a kettle so that I can make them a cup of tea. But I can't get the bread or make the cakes any more. They have to bring the cakes with them. It's not the same . . .

I've mixed with people all my life and I know we're all different. You've got learn to live with them. Some you're friends with straight away, some you wouldn't mix with, others you're not very certain about. But you can learn to get on with them. I believe Jesus loves us all so if he loves them then I can learn too.

I still see my friends on Sunday when Mr — picks me up for church. It's a bit difficult because I have to be back for lunch at 12.30, but sometimes I go out to lunch and that makes a nice change. It's not easy but if it's what God wants then it will work out. I believe that and it comforts me.

Whenever possible, church friends should try and visit frequently someone who has just gone into a home, even if there are family who visit. Most people need someone with whom they can share their troubles, and adjusting takes time. Family often cannot help. It needs someone who can be non-judgmental, who can help them find new ways of coping with the problems that arise, and gradually help them come to the point of acceptance.

Mrs Hegarty needed to go over again and again the pain of losing her own home, whilst recognising that there were good things about the new place. In the past she had done lots of embroidery, and it was possible for her to take that up again. She also did knitting and became much in demand by the care staff, making clothes for their children. She charged for the work and the money went to the church.

Close family members will also value support. Most families would like to care for their elderly relatives but it is often not a realistic option. Housing is so expensive that it is often impossible to buy somewhere suitable for several generations to live together, and it rarely works for noisy teenagers to be living in close proximity to someone sick or frail. Family frictions and unresolved conflicts from earlier days tend to surface again.

Even when families have decided together that residential care is the best option, they can still feel a lot of guilt and failure. This may show itself in a number of ways. Often relatives will appear hard and callous – they are afraid of criticism, so a wall goes up to prevent the possibility of rejection by other carers, home staff and the church. The non-involved helper may then feel left to cope. He or she should try not to resent it but recognise that relatives are facing a tremendous struggle. If they too are shown understanding in love, then later they may be able to visit their frail relative more frequently. Certainly showing disapproval will only widen the rift between everyone.

Even when family relationships are good, relatives are unlikely to be able to bear hearing about the frail person's difficulties. Mrs Hegarty had a very close relationship with her daughter and son-in-law, but she could not talk with them about adjusting to the home because they could not understand. They could only cope by seeing the home as a lovely place where Mrs Hegarty 'had everything she needed'. It is normal to need a friend and confidant who is slightly more detached, with whom to share personal feelings and pain.

Other relatives cope with their guilt by visiting the frail relative very frequently, wanting to do everything for them, resenting anything anyone else does and generally being very possessive. They may rebuff other friends and helpers, or see their concern as nosiness. It is important to try not to be hurt by this, and to continue to visit perhaps at times when the family will not be there. The frail person does need other contacts; and the time will come when the family visit less frequently and then the elderly person can feel very isolated. The relatives, too, will often, with time, come to appreciate genuine concern and be able to share some of their feelings with someone who knows the situation. They may have no one else to share them with.

For adult children, facing up to the frailty of their parents often arises through a crisis. Everyone else may have seen the slow deterioration but the elderly parents will generally want to remain independent and therefore hide many of their problems, so that generally the children have difficulty in facing the implications for themselves. It is never easy to become the oldest generation in any family.

CHAPTER 7

Frailty and Sickness

'Though the outer man is perishing the inner man is renewed day by day.' (2 Corinthians 4.16)

Paul wrote this to the Corinthian Christians in the context of his own suffering and exhaustion in the cause of the gospel. It can also be an encouragement to older Christians who are facing frailty and sickness.

Few people push their minds and bodies to the extent that Paul did. Certainly few, unless they are sports enthusiasts, need recognise any diminishing of skill or energy during adulthood, because age teaches everyone how to use physical, mental and emotional capacities less wastefully. There is plenty of scope to maintain mental and physical fitness for everyone who chooses to take the opportunities available. It can therefore be well into retirement before someone becomes aware that they are 'slowing down'. Even then it may be no more than a mild irritant for those who still feel fulfilled as people.

Mary finally retired when she was seventy, having previously cut her working week from five days to three days when she was sixty-five. Like over 50 per cent of the population she wore glasses, and had done since the age of twenty. She had recurrent problems with a chronic illnes which she had contracted during adolescence (although it rarely necessitated time off work). From her forties onwards she had bouts of colitis which she had learned to control by a sensible diet. She had arthritis in the big toe of her right foot, so she walked awkwardly. Apart from that she remained fit and healthy. She was a quietly active member of the local free evangelical church, attending services and prayer meetings, visiting housebound and sick people, doing the washing when someone was ill, encouraging mums whilst their children were going through the difficult teenage years. She did not finally retire until she was seventy, because the job, which was poorly paid, gave her no pension.

Retirement didn't bring much change to her life style – it just gave her more time to serve others and to spend time with her friends.

Her church had steadily decreased in numbers and she worried about where she would go if it closed down. She also dreaded the possibility of having to care for elderly relatives in the future.

At seventy-six she joined an archaeological society and was relishing the new interest it brought, even though during recent months she had felt increasingly tired and for the first time in her life wanted to take cat naps during the day.

A couple of months later she felt unwell and visited the doctor and then suddenly and unexpectedly early one morning a few days later she died.

If you think through the people you have known I think you will find many whose story is similar to Mary. Or look round your church at the lifestyles of those in their sixties, seventies, eighties and even nineties. Although the 'outer man has been perishing' this has been in a way unique to each individual. Yet books about ageing so often present a depressing picture, of increasing deafness, poor sight, deteriorated taste and smell, calcium deficiency, and so on. They are almost the modern equivalent of Ecclesiastes 12! This often happens because the books are written by people who see a disproportionate number of frail people in the course of their work.

Early in my working life I was a social worker with older people who were considering residential care. After about twelve years I transferred to community work with elderly people and I still remember the impact the change had on me as I realised how my view of old age had been negatively influenced by the very frail people I had been used to meeting. It is also important to recognise that each new generation of older people is fitter than the previous one and that it can be no more than an educated guess as to what old age is going to mean for future generations.

Even if you are over retirement age yourself you really cannot predict what your final years will be like. I have stressed all this because rightly particular attention needs to be paid to supporting the frail people in our fellowships. The Bible gives instructions about caring for the sick, supporting the weak, the fatherless and the orphan. But the danger of making them unnecessarily dependent must be avoided and dependence on God and interdependency between everyone needs to be fostered. Paul writes vividly about this in his second letter to the Corinthians:

Blessed be the God and Father of our Lod Jesus Christ, the Father of mercies and God of all comfort, who comforts us in all our affliction, so that we may be able to comfort those who are in any affliction, with the comfort with which we ourselves are comforted by God. For as we share abundantly in Christ's sufferings, so through Christ we share abundantly in comfort too. If we are afflicted, it is for your comfort and salvation; and if we are comforted, it is for your comfort, which you experience when you patiently endure the same sufferings that we suffer. Our hope for you is unshaken; for we know that as you share in our sufferings, you will also share in our comfort. (2 Corinthians 1.3–7)

Beware of equating old age with frailty! There are many people under sixty-five who are ill or handicapped, and many older who remain in good health. None of Mary's illnesses limited her before or after retirement; and many adults have physical weaknesses which are coped with by avoiding the things that cause trouble – for instance, migraine sufferers avoid the food which will trigger a headache; people with ulcers usually need to avoid acidy foods; those with back trouble avoid lifting heavy weights.

Reasons for Frailty

Suffering and ill health at all ages can have many different origins. It can come from a genetic weakness. At other times it comes from abusing the body in some way. Alice fractured a leg ski-ing. It was a complicated break and she was warned not to play strenuous sports. She did, had another accident and has been confined to a wheelchair for the last thirty years.

Others suffer because of someone else's sin. Arthur, a very sprightly eighty-six-year-old, was knocked down on a zebra crossing by a drunken driver. His leg was broken in several places and now he can only walk about a hundred yards and he has frequent bouts of pain.

Suffering can also come through refusal to accept God's will. Daniel knew that God wanted him to do less, but he fought against it. Finally, although unexpectedly, he had a heart attack.

But there is also the anguish, like that recorded in the book of Job where, from the human angle there appears no logical explanation for the suffering although I am sure there is from God's point of view.

Spiritual Perspectives to Suffering

Whatever the cause, pain and ill health, when approached from a Christian perspective, can become a real growth point in the spiritual life. Some people, now very elderly, grew up with the idea that ill health and suffering are always the direct result of sin. They can be heard to say, 'Why has God done it to me? I've never done anyone any harm.' The way they say it will give us clues as to how we should respond. It may be said with bitterness and resentment; as though living 'a good life' means it should always be an easy life. The question may reflect a basic negative attitude in the person and reflect a chip on their shoulder that they have carried for years, or it may be said in puzzlement with the person searching their minds for a rational reason.

Our response will vary in each situation, but we need to be aware of two dangers. We must avoid being triumphalistic – assuming that God always provides easy answers and all we need to do is praise him! People should be encouraged by being reminded of the promises of God. We can discover how people in the Bible overcame their suffering; but we need to beware of glibness and to 'stay with' a sick person who is struggling to reach the kind of freedom Paul had when he was under house arrest in Rome (which comes through vividly in his letter to the Philippians). Or ultimately as Jesus showed on the cross. The opposite danger is to suggest that there is no way out and the person just has to 'grin and bear it'. We need to encourage the person to see that they can know God more deeply through what is happening.

A sick person may need encouragement to forgive others who may in part have caused their suffering; to trust God through seeing the indications he gives of his love and presence with them; to thank him for what he is providing – perhaps in the form of people to visit and care. It is so easy to take one's eyes off God and on to one's own circumstances when racked with pain and handicap. A concerned Christian friend can help a suffering fellow-Christian so much by praying with and for them so that they see what God is doing, and also by sharing passages of Scriptures as they seem to meet the need – Psalm 34 and 55, for example, which I develop in a little more detail in the second part of the book (see especially pages 166–72). Joni Eareckson, a quadriplegic, in *A Step Further*[1] points out that we are never alone even if we live in a flat and have few visitors. Joni's story is one that might help some to work through the challenge of their own handicap.

If a person is very ill and seems unconscious, it is important to visit and pray with them – hearing is one of the last senses to go. I was told a beautiful story of a visit to a hospital by a theological student. She was told to go to someone called Gladys who, although conscious, was considered out of touch with everything. She sat by the bedside, took Gladys's hand, explained who she was and why she was there, and spoke about what was happening on the ward. Then she sat quietly for a few minutes and let God's love flow through her to Gladys. Then she read a small passage from the Bible, prayed for Gladys's relatives (she had found out a little about them from the ward sister) and finally for Gladys herself. She sat again quietly for a minute or two. As she released her hand, Gladys made her first and only movement – she drew a cross with her finger on the student's hand.

Coping Psychologically with Suffering

But the spiritual battle with suffering is not the only aspect. There is also the psychological side. Both feelings and behaviour are affected by illness. Many older people rarely talk about feelings – that is a relatively recent fashion – but tend to talk much more in terms of actions – bad temperedness, self-pity, impatience, intolerance, cutting oneself off from others or being unrealistically demanding and attention-seeking. Underlying all this can be the fear of rejection. Whilst struggling to come to terms with suffering, old ways of behaving will tend to come back – for instance a short-tempered person is likely to become even more short-tempered or demanding. Gradually, if the situation is accepted, the person returns to normal.

Suffering generally has one of two effects – it either leads to more gentleness, understanding and compassion or it leads to hardness and more bitterness. The job of the helper is to stand alongside others and where possible help them to use suffering constructively. Refusal to accept reality leads to cynicism, misery and loneliness; and isolation follows as no one wants to visit or befriend them.

Psychologically it is like walking a tightrope – bad behaviour (or feelings if the person talks in feeling terms) needs to be acknowledged and some acceptable way of expressing it found, whilst at the same time the temptation to give in and wallow in the negative feeling or behaviour has to be avoided. It is a balance that varies for each person, and on each occasion. For the Christian, penitence, forgiveness and prayer are gifts that can and should be drawn on; but often one is called upon to stand alongside people who have no faith. Obviously we should still pray for them, and God will be seen to answer our prayers – although not necessarily in the way expected!

When anyone is faced with ill health, such as arthritis, a stroke, limited mobility after a heart attack, or cancer, there is generally an initial sense of disbelief and then sometimes denial which is really a form of rebellion – a refusal to accept facts because of the real or imaginary implication which the illness may have for the future. There is the inevitable sense of powerlessness and therefore of lack of control over life. A caring helper needs to walk patiently with the person until they are able to face, or are forced by circumstances to accept, the reality of their illness. The emotions then expressed may be more vehement because they have been bottled up. Frustration, impatience and intolerance are also common reactions, and then the person needs friends who are not rebuffed by their behaviour but able to go on caring, giving them the opportunity to share their feelings and their fears if they want to.

Others will react to the knowledge of illness with panic, and imagine the worst, or perhaps get everything out of proportion; they will need help to gain a sense of perspective. Another reaction can be to stop bothering about things – maybe becoming very depressed and perhaps refusing to co-operate with treatment or with people trying to help them. An extreme form of this is when people take to their beds.

Ideally there is finally a move on to acceptance of the situation which is causing the suffering. But acceptance does not mean giving in, nor is it a resigned acceptance of the inevitable. It is having a realistic view of the extent of one's own suffering, a willingness to limit its effects and, in embracing it, to continue to live life as fully as possible.

There is therefore a practical side to its acceptance.

Coping With the Practicalities

Today there are many ways of limiting the practical effects of illness. Operations and medical treatments are available for a vast range of diseases. Social services departments, voluntary and private agencies, provide a wide range of services to enable people to make the most of their own disabilities. It is difficult to keep up with all that is available and who is providing it (see Appendix C).

Bert's stroke affected the right side of his body. Whilst he was in hospital the physiotherapist taught him how to talk, to get in and out of an armchair and exercise himself so that he would remain as fit as possible and gradually gain more use from his partially paralysed arm and leg.

The hospital fitted a special shoe with a spring on it to help him walk. Before he left hospital the occupational therapist arranged for a chair lift to be installed at home because he needed to climb stairs to the bedroom, bathroom and toilet. Bert enjoyed playing cards and writing letters so she also showed him a catalogue of aids to help him with daily living activities and with her advice he chose special playing cards, a holder, pens and a writing frame. She also arranged grab rails for the bath and around the toilet. Sadly, at the moment because of his anger against God, Bert is unwilling to use some of the aids and instead sits in the chair much of the time, biting his wife's head off.

Spouses and Children

When someone is ill the greatest burden falls on the carer, and with a married couple this is normally the partner (who is more likely to be the wife as women tend to outlive men by two or three years on average). On the whole, social services (like the home help, district nurses, etc.) are most likely to be given to those living alone, so that the burden of care on an elderly spouse can be very heavy and demanding, especially as the carer may have decreasing energy to cope.

Bert's wife Alice was feeling very stressed, not only by the physical care he needed but by the emotional demands he made. Just how burdened she felt it was difficult to know because, typical of her generation, but probably even more because of their over sixty years of happy marriage, loyalty forbade her complaining, and naturally I did not question her.

Alice had to reorganise her life completely when Bert came out of hospital. He went to out-patients for physiotherapy twice each week and she had to get him up at 6.30 am so that he was ready for the ambulance which was due at nine but could arrive as late as ten. He got annoyed when he had to wait. He could arrive back any time from one o'clock onwards and needing lunch. Coping with the stroke exhausted him, and his anger and resentment drained his energy still further, so that he wanted to be in bed early in the evening. He demanded that Alice go to bed at the same time.

During the day he always wanted to know what she was doing and wanted endless cups of tea, which necessitated frequent trips to the toilet. As he was unsteady on his feet she had to go with him. The amount of washing increased because he couldn't always make the toilet in time.

To have to cope with a new routine at eighty-four in addition to the distress of seeing the person you love most in the world struggling mentally, physically and spiritally is distressing.

Although Bert stopped going to church, the church didn't stop going to him. Fortunately there were two men in the church willing to visit him, although he would not accept visits from the priest. But Alice had to give up going to her Mothers' Union meeting.

Supporting Relatives and Carers

Helping the carers of the elderly sick person may be far from easy. They are often reluctant to ask for help and frequently are not sure what help people are willing to give. Helpers are afraid of intruding!

It is essential that help is consistent and reliable, and as far as possible it is better to help in ways that cannot be covered by other means. Sometimes it can be something quite simple. I remember a wife saying to me many years ago that what she and her husband would like more than anything was to be taken out together for an afternoon in the countryside – not as a special arrangement but just with people who were going out anyway. Or the homes of housebound people could be used for meetings for Bible study and prayer. Sometimes taking the washing to the launderette and doing the ironing once a week is the most useful way of helping. Shopping locally can be very expensive, so giving someone a lift when you are going to the supermarket, or offering to get shopping for them, are other possibilities. Spending a couple of hours on a regular basis with the sick person sharing a mutual hobby so that the active partner can get out for a break will be appreciated.

Sensitivity is needed in offering to pray with either the sick person or the partner, or both. Where prayer for each other is a normal part of church life it is worth being bold and asking whether they would like you to pray or read the Bible with them during your visit. Where it is not part of church life then it is better to discuss their likely response with people in the church who know them well.

You may know frail people whose lives might be eased. In Appendix C there is a list of some of the services of professional people available and the type of help they provide. If you do not know who to turn to, with the sick person's consent ask the advice of their general practitioner or the social services department social worker.

CHAPTER 8

Mental Health and Illness in Later Life

In Chapter 1, I mentioned the tendency to stereotype older people and use negative adjectives about them. Professional workers can all too often be heard to refer to them as the 'geriatrics'. Not infrequently a person of over ninety may refer to someone of seventy living down the road as 'old and past it!' Old is something other people can be, but it is not something that we want to claim for ourselves! That in itself shows just how negative our attitude to old age can be. Margaret, at ninety-two, said, 'I don't feel any different to when I was forty. I know I've got wrinkles and can't walk very far, but I still watch the news and go to a current affairs adult education class each week.' The real problem is that old age is assumed to be a time of forgetfulness, of decline and of long-term ill health. The facts give a different picture.

The memory is a very complicated structure, and how it works is still not really understood, but current research seems to indicate that most of our memory functions do not deteriorate with age. Certainly the traditionally held views are untrue – people who are absent-minded in old age were absent-minded when young! It only becomes obvious when there isn't a secretary to remind them of what they've forgotten! A very severely handicapped medical social worker once said to me, 'You become more aware of your forgetfulness when it becomes an effort to put right what you've forgotten!' The illustration she gave was of leaving a bag upstairs. When we are agile we go up for it without thinking twice. When it becomes an effort our forgetfulness is drawn to our attention.

There is a common idea that ageing leads to problems with concentration. Studies done over a period of years show that changes are related to whether or not concentration continues to be practised. Also, the length of time that a person can attend to one thing alone varies enormously – no doubt for many churchgoers, listening to long sermons every week gives high scores in any test of concentration. Another common, but mistaken view, is that intelligence reduces with age. It doesn't. The ability to absorb and use information, and to understand the world, does not change. As at any age, it depends on natural skills and the willingness and openness to go on learning. But it should be remembered that all skills that are not used for any length of time go rusty!

Neither do people need to become 'turned in on themselves'. There are those who will, because they choose to give in to their already narcissistic tendencies. There is also the danger, particularly with those who become housebound, of being pressed into unhealthy preoccupation with themselves through not being provided with stimulating interests and relationships.

Old age, then, has no need to conform to the current negative images. Ageism is rampant enough in our society – not least within our churches. The fact that we meet old pepole who have become turned in on themselves, who are inflexible and who insist they are forgetful and cannot concentrate as they once did, who claim they are not as intelligent as they were, all shows how detrimental subjective attitudes can be to well-being. How sad to waste what could be up to fifteen or more years of life!

But where there is true forgetfulness, loss of memory, and so on, these are symptoms of physical or mental illness which need diagnosing and, if possible, treatment. Personality disorders and neuroses continue to affect about 10 per cent of people over sixty-five – a similar percentage to those in younger age groups. Depression affects another 10 per cent; but perhaps the statistic which is most surprising is that the 'dementias' affect only 3.2 per cent of people over sixty-five and yet these receive the most publicity!

Personality Disorders and Neuroses

These are terms applied to a kind of 'catch all' category of people whom others believe to be abnormal in some way. They are used to describe people with obsessions, generalised anxiety which significantly affects their everday living, those who behave in an immature way for their years, are unable to control their anger, have alcohol problems, behave antisocially, are over-dependent, manipulative, have irrational fears, and so on.

I guess all of us can recognise one or more of these types of behaviour in ourselves; but from a psychiatrist's point of view they are only considered an illness when they cause major problems to the person concerned or to people around them. There is no evidence at all that the likelihood of personality disorder increases with age. Such disorders are usually of long standing. And sometimes, inexplicably, they can suddenly disappear.

Emma was totally dependent on her husband, spent much of each day in bed because she insisted she had a weak heart, and expected her two children, her sister, her niece and her husband to dance attendance all the time. Everyone though she would be the first to die. Instead, she outlived them all, and a while after the death of her final relative – a niece – when she was seventy-five, confounded her neighbours and professional workers by starting to look after herself completely, running her home effectively and going out and meeting people! She finally died some twelve years later, never having reverted to her dependent behaviour.

Elderly people can be helped with the milder personality problems that most people have in the same ways as anyone else. The real key is whether or not they want to change. If they do, then God's resources are available to them. It must be borne in mind that, since any habit becomes more ingrained the longer it is practised, it will take longer for new healthy attitudes and forms of behaviour to take its place. This means that older peole will need a lot of encouragement, and the steps in bringing about the change may need to be smaller and slower. However, where the disorder or neurosis appears for the first time in old age (and where it does not relate to some specific illness or dementia, or drug treatment) then it is no more difficult or easy to break than for a younger person.

Personality Problems in Older People

Where the problem is a long-term one and the person has no wish to change, there is little that can be done, even by a psychiatrist. The person often displays manipulative behaviour towards others. The problem can be worsened by the feeling on the part of would-be helpers that they should not be firm with an elderly or frail person. It is not long before the person has the helper running round in circles after them, or avoiding them altogether. It really is important that the helper is firm over what he or she is not willing to do. And others must stand by them, or the frail person will start playing one person off against the other! You have probably experienced it!

James was confined to a wheelchair because of a stroke. He had had a lot of help with adjusting psychologically to his handicap. He was very demanding and strong-willed. He had a home help who came on a Friday morning to do his shopping. However he preferred her to do the washing.

At about 5 pm he would ring someone in the church requesting them to take him shopping to the local supermarket, and always insisted on going with them. The shopping done, after a long queue at the check-out he would say how lonely he was and could they just get some fish and chips and eat it with him. Eventually the helper would arrive home at about 10 pm. After three or four weeks the helper would say 'No', James would then go on to someone else! Because people didn't talk about their 'good deed' it was a good eighteen months before anyone realised what was happening, and then tales of his other demands began coming out. All the time he could have been making use of the health and social services personnel – instead he was using them to do jobs he could do himself!

Studies which show that 10 per cent of elderly people suffer from depression are referring to much more than sadness, moodiness, or the general 'down in the dumps' feeling that everyone experiences from time to time and is often called depression. A person with clinical depression – to use its technical name – needs treatment from a doctor. Where a person suffers from it for the first time in old age it will often be treated by drugs with very successful results.

The outcome is much less good when there is a repeated history of depression earlier in life. It is important however to remember that depression always eventually lifts; but it can last for several years. Drugs shorten the time dramatically. Whenever anyone seems depressed they should be encouraged to see a doctor, as it is the most easily treated of all mental illness. But there is much that can be done to prevent someone from reaching the stage of needing medical help.

There are numerous causes for depression – in elderly people it may be caused by the drugs needed for some physical illness, or by isolation, it can be a natural phase of bereavement or occur during adustment to handicap such as a stroke. At all ages it can arise from repressed anger, negative thinking, feelings of helplessness or insecurity, guilt, low self-esteem, perfectionism, poor eating or sleeping habits or reaction to prolonged stress.

In helping someone who feels depressed, whether they are being treated by a doctor or not, it is important to recognise what is the underlying cause – or 'trigger'. When depression arises from external reasons, as when, for instance, the person feels they do not have enough contact with other people, then we must look for ways of meeting that need.

When depression is a result of disrupted eating or sleeping habits then people can be encouraged to regain an appropriate pattern; portions of favourite food taken as gifts, invitations out to meals or being asked to prepare tea or simple snacks for visitors can help.

Guilt can be a major cause of depression, particularly where it keeps recurring in cycles. Guilt arises from a sense of sin. It can be handled in three ways – one helpful, two unhelpful. An attempt can be made to try to repress or deny it. This then leads to feelings of anger, rebellion, fear, anxiety and on to a deadening of conscience and increasing aggression. On the other hand with introspective people, guilt may be acknowledged and then result in despair and depression.

Guilt, though is God's way of bringing us to repentance. If you know someone who is feeling guilty you need to help them admit to God the reason for the guilt and then accept his forgiveness. On pages 122 and 166–8, I have suggested ways of handling the situation when it is more complicated.

A sense of worthlessness, of being unwanted, of not being allowed to give to others, also leads to depression – and these are common causes in old age. In an earlier chapter I suggested that older people are undervalued and denigrated in our society and too often in the church as well. Love can exist only when there is freedom and the willingness to both give and receive. Older people are denied the right to love when they are denied the right to give. Underlying Paul's beautiful picture of the Body of Christ in 1 Corinthians 12 is the fact that everyone is gifted by God to give to his Body, the Church, and needs to receive from others the gifts God has given them through the head of the Body who is Christ.

In eastern religions old age is seen as the time of withdrawal from society and a concentration on prayer and the life to come. Sometimes this idea is recommended to Christians. I can find no biblical justification for it – especially as a life of concentrated prayer is a particularly stressful calling. Great thought needs to be taken before suggesting that older housebound saints can do the praying for the rest of us in the church. Of course prayer must be the foundation of the life of every Christian and most of us find it a very difficult activity. When someone is asked to take on a heavy weight of prayer when it is not their gift, and where there is not a sensitive understanding of the dynamics of prayer, the resulting marginalisation, sense of uselessness and failure can lead people into deep depression.

Depression can also come as a natural stage in bereavement, in adjusting to ill health and in reviewing the events of life and these issues are explored in Chapters 8 and 11.

Anger, when it is bottled up, can also lead to depression. It is often easy to see a cycle – anger, bitterness, cynicism, judgmentalism, refusal to forgive and a longing for revenge; when no revenge is possible then depression follows. In younger life people often channel their anger into some form of campaigning for the rights of others as a form of justification for their own unacknowledged anger. This may no longer be possible when they become old. Behind the anger there are usually feelings of hurt, fear, and frustration – and older people could be said to to be justified in having these feelings. However, justification only compounds the problem. Freedom can only come from forgiving the people who have caused the pain, frustration or fear. Again if anger is a more recent response to problems, then it is an easier habit to break than if it is an automatic response.

There is a further specific type of depression called endogenous depression. Whilst medical experts argue over the use of the term it nevertheless identifies a depression which 'comes over' a person without there being any reasonable explanation; it is the result of a chemical imbalance in the brain. It usually appears in young people and the only treatment is drugs. It is not curable by human means and tends to worsen as people get older.

Helping People who are Depressed

If you know someone who is severely depressed, the first and most important thing is a willingness to show that you really care and want to understand: listening, perhaps again and again to the tale of woe; certainly visiting, or inviting them to visit you regularly. Understanding them may be difficult. The person, themselves, may not understand what is happening to them.

A sense of failure often looms large. Older people tend to mix less with others, and spend more time watching television and listening to the radio where the news reinforces their gloom and negativity! Some people just want to wallow, and their choice must be respected, but most will welcome help to get out of the rut. This will not be too difficult when people have previously been positive and outgoing, but where their past lives have been marked by negativity and pessimism, change will be slow.

Habits of a lifetime do not change overnight!

But one is never too old to change, and the Holy Spirit is a lovely, gentle teacher, if feelings and behaviour are given to him.

Try to help people to see the positives in a situation, however small, to avoid blanket negative statements like 'I can't cope' and to turn negative comments into factual statements.

Try and encourage people to mix. Go on inviting them to church functions. Even if at first they say no, they may change their mind at a later date.

Do encourage them to read their Bibles, and it may act as an incentive if you suggest discussing passages together. They may find prayer difficult but many older Christians will welcome someone praying with them even when they feel unable to pray for themselves. Depression nearly always has a spiritual dimension – guilt, unforgiveness, lack of trust in God, sin – and I have mentioned these issues on pages 166–72. I have also listed one or two books which deal with the subject of depression in more detail.[1]

Increased forgetfulness and confusion is a common symptom of depression with older people. It can be very difficult to see the difference between that and 'a dementia', so skilled medical diagnosis is very important as early as possible.

'Dementia'

Were you surprised earlier in the chapter to discover that only 3.2 per cent of people over sixty-five suffer from 'dementia'? Yet understandably it is probably the disease many of us are most frightened of. Dementia is a general term given to several different conditions but there are two main ones which affect older people – senile dementia (also known as Alzheimer's disease) and arteriosclerotic dementia. Very little is known about either disease and more research is badly needed, but neither appears to be hereditary.

Senile dementia arises from changes in the brain's cell structure, the reasons for which are unknown. The disease comes on very gradually – perhaps over several years. However it often seems sudden, for example, when a person 'goes to pieces' after a change in their surroundings. Changes seem to highlight the underlying deterioration. Usually the person is unaware of anything being wrong although those around them will become very distressed at the changes in their personality and behaviour. Responses become blunted very early and sufferers often show complete lack of understanding and consideration for others. Sometimes a previously gentle person becomes aggressive and foul-mouthed.[2]

The other form of dementia – arteriosclerotic (also known as multi-farct) dementia – is caused by a disruption of the blood supply to the brain. Instead of gradual deterioration there are sudden episodes of deterioration – with a big increase in the person's level of confusion – then some improvement, a plateau, and then another deterioration. To begin with the deterioration is 'patchy' – impairing speech, or behaviour or orientation separately according to the part of the brain affected.

Unlike the early deterioration seen in senile dementia the personality of someone with arteriosclerotic dementia often remains relatively unaffected for some time. This can cause enormous distress because the person is then aware of their deteriorating condition – inability to remember certain things, or to cope with some activities that require a lot of thought or co-ordination. To begin with, recent events are not remembered, but gradually medium and distant memories cannot be recalled either. People tend to 'cover up' for their specific memory losses but realistic fears of losing control of their reason can lead to severe depression, or frustration or violence towards others.

Other symptoms of both senile and arteriosclerotic dementia include: 1) speech problems – inability to select the right word, although they know what they want to say; inability to name familiar objects; meaningless repetition of phrases, or inability to understand questions; 2) lack of co-ordination leading to clumsy gait, an inability to dress, wash properly or do household jobs; 3) loss of bladder control; 4) turning night into day by reversal of sleep patterns; 5) agitated behaviour or wandering.

People with either type of dementia are helped by familiar routines, experiencing as few changes as possible. For example, it is wise not to introdcue new gadgets, such as an electric safety kettle, unless it is absolutely necessary and it is certain that the person really can use it and not be confused still further. Neither is it helpful for them to be taken to unfamiliar places unnecessarily – it only increases their confusion.

Supporting Elderly People
who Become Confused or Mentally Frail

Whenever 'confusion' or 'depression', or any change in an older person's personality appears, the first essential is to encourage them to go their doctor, who will hopefully refer them on to either a

111

geriatrician (a hospital consultant specialising in the physical diseases of old age) or to a psychiatrist who specialises in mental health and illness in old age. Both are used to visiting people in their own homes and to making their diagnoses on an out-patient basis. You can reassure the elderly person that (unless they are very ill) hospital admission is unlikely. Naturally, older people are particularly fearful of referral to a psychiatrist. The problem is that the diagnosis and treatment of depression and the dementias demands a lot of skill, and few general practitioners have it. Yet a wrong diagnosis can mean years of quite unnecessary misery. If there are no relatives available, the person may be helped by an offer to be there when the GP or specialist visits, or to take them to hospital for their out-patient's appointment.

Only on rare occasions should any action be taken without the agreement of the person concerned, and only then if the helper feels they are doing what the old person would want if they were 'in their right mind'.

Esther, a very difficult, independent, housebound old lady of ninety-four, sometimes forget she had put the kettle on the stove, and burned through the bottom! She had always been distrustful of people. Then one day in October she insisted there were bugs crawling over the dining room walls, which she was adamant came from her neighbour's house. The next day she put jam on her potatoes and salt in her tea. By the next day she was wrongly dressed, slip over her dress, slippers on the wrong feet and she was busy scrubbing the walls with talcum powder.

Friends called the doctor, although she protested. He happened to be a locum as it was her

112

usual doctor's day off. He said that it was 'just old age', and that it was only her normal behaviour accentuated. He advised them to call a social worker to get her admitted to a home. By a couple of days later she was very lethargic; she had turned the central heating off saying she was hot, was sleeping during the day and wandering round at night. Then her regular doctor, having been notified of the emergency visit, recognised that something was seriously wrong. He visited and arranged immediate admission to hospital where she was found to have mild hypothermia (low body temperature). When that was treated they felt that she had been, and still was, moderately depressed, so mild anti-depressants were prescribed. By the next summer, with practical support and encouragement from church friends and a home help, Esther was much more cheerful and almost back to her previous level of independence.

Esther had no close relatives, but her friends knew she would normally accept a doctor's visit so they felt it right to call one. Their action was later vindicated.

When she came out of hospital someone from the church visited daily to begin with to make sure she was all right. The car lifts to services restarted and two scouts went in each fortnight to do her garden and any odd jobs that needed doing.

Everyone is brighter at some parts of the day that at others. I am half asleep until about 10 am, benefit from an afternoon snooze and am at my brightest in the late evening. Others will be the 'rise and shine' type but be ready for bed by 10 pm. People with depression, senile or arterio-sclerotic dementia also have varying capacities for concentration throughout the day. It is always worth working out when they are most lucid and arranging visits for those times.

Unless you know the person well you will probably find it easiest to visit in pairs and if you are unsure how to cope, try to visit with someone who has experience and a gift for getting along with people with bad memories.

When people become agitated it helps to do something active with them on your visits – take them for a walk, or do some cleaning together. Sometimes they can be distracted and then it is helpful to know what normally interests them. Where there has been a lively Christian faith, singing some of their favourite hymns and choruses can change their mood and calm them.

It is amazing how some people with whom it has become impossible to hold a normal conversation can still remember how to play the piano, or use skills gained years before; it is worthwhile trying to find out about any talents or hobbies a person may have had when younger, and see if these can again be a means of enjoyment and interest.

Do not be put off, when visiting a friend who is mentally confused, if every time you go you are unrecognised and may at first be rejected. Just think for a moment about what they are facing. Imagine yourself sitting in your favourite armchair by the fire, snoozing. Suddenly you are awoken by two strangers saying they have come to chat to you. What is your reaction? Or there is a ring at the door, and when you go there is a stranger there saying she has come to take you to Sunday service. You are sure it's 5 pm on Monday. What is your reaction?

These are the types of situation that people with poor memories due to illness are faced with daily. If you felt frightened, threatened, angry, confused, just imagine what it is like for them. It's amazing really how accepting people are. But be patient with repeatedly explaining who you are, where you have come from and why you are there. Do persevere in your visits and help, as you are providing a very important service in helping the person to maintain what abilities they still have.

Most people, though, have some memory – often for earlier events in their lives. Some enjoy endlessly repeating the same ones, others do so because they cannot think or remember anything else to say; still others because they are trying to keep in touch with themselves. Except for the first group it can help if you try to get a person to remember the event that happened immediately after the memory they have recalled. For example, someone talks about their wedding – you could then go on to ask about the birth of their first child (if they had one), what the child was like as a baby. Or if they are talking about the death of King George V, you could then ask about the abdication of Edward VIII. In this way you gradually bring them further forward in time. Getting them to talk about old photographs can also sometimes help. Church photos and memorabilia are invaluable with people whose church has been the bedrock of their lives. Photos of them taken at recent events can also be used successfully. Do not necessarily expect them to remember quickly; there is usually quite a delay between a distant memory being triggered and its vividness coming to mind. So with mentally infirm people it may be necessary to provide the trigger many times before a glimmer of memory appears.

Insisting that a dead person is still alive can be a particularly stressful habit with some people. Do not encourage the idea that what they say is true – it only confuses their deep inner memories all the more. On the other hand avoid making an issue out of their incorrect statement. If you can, gently correct the statement, saying something like, 'Your mother died twenty years ago in 1970. Now you're living here at — by yourself . . . Shall we have a cup of tea?'

Sometimes a confused person may insist on going out, perhaps looking for someone, even though it is freezing cold, or pouring with rain. If you cannot divert their attention easily it is better to agree to go out with them but gradually focus on the going out itself rather than the reason. You will usually find that after a few minutes walk they are happy to return home.

Where there is a Christian faith, do read and pray with them. If they enjoy the modern Bible versions, songs and prayers, fine – but if they prefer, or seem to relate more easily to the King James Bible and old hymns, use them. If they are used to the Book of Common Prayer, the Latin Mass or the Angelus, use those. These are what gave them comfort at a previous stage of their lives; it is these which God is most likely to use to speak to them now.

Using 'thou' prayers rather than 'you' prayers may be more acceptable. If you come from a church used to praying for people's healing and having a deliverance ministry, you may long to pray with them. Try to remember that in most non-pentecostal churches God has only recently released these gifts, and most old people will find this type of prayer frightening and threatening. This is especially so if they have dementia. Most of the praying should go on without the person being present. As in all situations, the praying group needs to wait on God to hear clearly how they should pray and what they should pray for. Prayer with the person should always grow out of a deep love and respect for them. There is no place for aggressive, authoritarian deliverance commands. In praying for the sufferer be as gentle as you would in praying with a tiny baby. But do pray. I believe that God wants us to use his gifts of healing. I have seen enough people healed of depression to believe that he also wants to heal those with dementia. But I believe too, that he also longs to bring peace to people who are tormented, even though for some reason we do not see their minds and brains restored. Deliverance may, on occasion, be called for especially where someone has had an unhealthy life style prior to the illness developing, and therefore be vulnerable to the devil's attacks. But a deliverance ministry is not to be approached lightly, and should always be undertaken by someone with experience and a special gift for this type of ministry. It can extremely dangerous if attempted by a well-meaning, but inexperienced and ungifted person. It also seems to me that it is against all the Bible teaches us about God that he would allow Christians who, because of mental frailty are unable to defend themselves against the devil's temptations, to become the devil's victims. Remember, God set the boundaries of the devil's activities in respect of Job.

Supporting Relatives

Dementia is very distressing for those who have known the person before they became ill. There is a sense of powerlessness to do anything but watch the deterioration in personality and ability to cope. The strain of caring can become increasingly heavy. The person may be so restless or irresponsible as to need constant attention, or their unpredictable behaviour may become a social embarrassment in company, so that relatives can become increasingly isolated. Often repetitive behaviour makes relatives very impatient and frustrated and then they feel guilty and ashamed. Relatives get no thanks or appreciative comments from the sick person to encourage them. Some relatives care out of a sense of duty, others out of love for the people the afflicted once were.

Care and support from concerned Christians can make all the difference between relatives continuing to care for the frail person at home and becoming so exhausted that the person needs to enter hospital or a home. It is important to separate the needs of the frail person and of the carer. Make sure too, that if the aim is to befriend both, that one or other does not lose out. Generally, if the sufferer is very frail, it is easier if some people concentrate on caring for the frail person whilst others support the relatives.

However, if you are visiting a mentally ill person, the relative must be able to rely on you visiting on the days and time you say. If you intend to visit casually then ring up beforehand to check that it is convenient. Regular visiting allows the carers to organise their time better. If they know you will be there, they may want the opportunity to go shopping or to have a rest. Never pass judgement on the carer – the frail person, particularly in the earlier stages of dementia, may present a false picture of how well they cope or what is happening. The person with depression may be transferring their feelings on to their carers. Always remember the Christian responsibility to build bridges between people, not build walls. Ask the carers what will be most helpful. Give them time to unburden their frustrations, dilemmas, maybe conflicts between providing for the frail person and for other family members. Again and again, carers say that what they need is someone who will sit and listen to them. You may not be able to offer any positive answers but feeling that someone understands helps. Needless to say because the carer can feel much guilt and often has feelings of disloyalty in talking about the sick person both a non-judgmental attitude and complete confidentiality are essential.[3]

There may be practical ways in which you can help. Taking the carer shopping, or sitting up on the occasional night when the frail person is particularly restless or disturbed. Taking the frail person out for a few hours to give them a break. Or sleeping in for a couple of nights whilst the carer has a weekend away. Pray with the relative. If you demonstate to the carer your willingness to be flexible over practical help then you will be able to do an enormous amount to prevent the carer breaking under the strain. Health authorities, social service departments, voluntary organisations and, increasingly, private agencies provide services for people who are mentally frail but their extent and quality varies enormously from place to place. Financial help – like the attendance allowance – may also be available through state benefits. But as things change it is best to consult the local Citizens Advice Bureau, giving an outline of the situation and asking what people and services the carer might contact.

Unfortunately services are rarely flexible, so it is often a question of help not exactly meeting the need. Sometimes it can mean that the help available really is not relevant. This is where a caring church can do so much. Relatives will also usually find it supportive to be in touch with the Carers' National Association and the Alzheimer's Disease Society – addresses in Appendix D.

CHAPTER 9

Dying, Death and Bereavement

Many books have been written on these subjects in the last few years. Here I am going to concentrate only on aspects which are either particularly important in old age or not relevant to people of younger age groups and thus are not generally covered in other books.

Facing the End of Life in This World

Those experienced in the care of the dying suggest that, when death is faced by a person after the diagnosis of terminal illness, there is usually a recognisable pattern of adjustment. The initial reaction is one of denial, which is followed by anger, bargaining, depression and finally acceptance over a period of months.

However, many elderly people I have known have not shown that kind of pattern. I suspect there are at least four reasons for this.

1. With longer experience of life, the ability to cope grows as familiarity also grows. Older people have generally had a lot of experience of seeing other people die and so become less fearful about their own death and are able to move through more easily to acceptance and serenity.
2. Death is the inevitable, and therefore predictable, end to old age.
3. For some, life can have become very tiring and therefore death comes as a welcome relief.
4. For Christians there is also a fourth reason.

There is the knowledge and the expectancy of meeting Jesus face to face. For many like Jane (in Chapter 2), God has become a familiar companion and so the moment of death will be no more than a change of surroundings. But this can only come when nothing in life has been hidden from God or left unforgiven.

For these reasons, acceptance of one's own death in old age tends to be a gradual process and is achieved in the midst of life, rather than when someone has been told that they do not have all that long to live.

Coping with the Past

Working towards accepting death means also accepting all that has happened during one's life; to see it as completed and as having sense to it. Guilt can be a real cause of someone's fear of death. I guess all of us know people whose lives are bound by guilt. Unlike younger people, older Christians, once we get to know them well, are generally much more willing to share their sense of guilt – which is often about a failure to live up to Christ's standards. It can also be about specific events. Guilt is a God-given gift, because without it we can never come to the point of repentance and thus receive God's forgiveness which releases us not only from our sin but from the guilt of our sin. Guilt leads to despair. Forgiveness leads to joy.

When older people are looking back over their lives they can have a sense of failure – and thus guilt – because they have not achieved what they felt was their potential. For some this is a fair assessment, but for others the standards they set themselves may have been quite unrealistic. For those whose failure is real, repentance can never come too late, because God's forgiveness can release their potentialities. But there must be a reason for the blockage. I find that it helps the person if they talk through the reasons in detail and then ask God for forgiveness for all the individual sins that make up the whole failure. Roman Catholics, Anglo Catholics and Greek Orthodox Christians will then normally want and benefit from confession to a priest. Others, who believe in the 'priesthood of all believers' and in the complete authority of Scripture will be helped by having one or more of the promises of Scripture read or prayed over them after their confession to God.

Another particular problem area for the present generation of older people is the legacy of the 1939–45 war. A few may not have been greatly affected, but many will have experienced the deaths of relatives, friends and neighbours. Some will still be harbouring anger (which by now is frequently eating their insides out!) against the 'offending' nation, particularly Germany or Japan. We see this hatred breaking out when there is a Nazi war trial, or the death of a country's leader who made decisions that led to the cruel deaths. Some people have never been able to let go of their hatred and vengeance and to forgive the offenders. The result is that they have been unable to release their loved one, and what began as a 'hardening of the heart' in one situation has led to a personality distorted in many ways. Just how this problem works itself out will vary from person to person. It is both hard for us as helpers to handle and for the person concerned, because it is a hatred that started so many years ago. It is not helped by a church or society which has lost the ability to recognise that forgiveness does not mean that the offence, or sin, is swept under the carpet. Forgiveness means saying, 'Yes, I know that you did . . . but nevertheless I forgive you.' It means asking God to forgive the offence and leaving him free to bring the offender or offending nation to the point of repentance and restitution.[1]

Another issue concerned with the war which often emerges in old age is the knowledge for some people that as soldiers, seamen or airmen they were responsible for killing other people. British war films obviously focus on the daring and bravery that took place, but as you watch the next film just think how that 'hero' might feel now if he thinks of how many lives he cut short. Many people will be able to handle the issue philosophically in a variety of ways, but those who are sensitive, or to whom God shows a different perspective, the result can be devastating. Some, too, were responsible for atrocities that were no better than those committed by the troops and civilians of other countries. Many will be helped by someone sharing their prayer of repentance and ministering God's forgiveness. They may also need to place their heavy burden at the foot of the cross. Their feelings will be very mixed and they will probably need help to identify them. These may include anger at their leaders for forcing them into compromising situations; fear at their lack of self-control; feelings of helplessness; shame at their behaviour; worthlessness as they recognise the full extent of what they were capable of doing; guilt at the number of other people's lives they ruined, and so on. Various 'layers' of the memory will gradually surface. It is unlikely that it will all come out at once. Gentleness and compassion on the part of the listener are of the utmost importance.

Some people find it difficult to find anything good in their lives and the high point may be something which seems insignificant to us. With men I find this frequently refers to the war.

Charlie was called up in 1940 at the age of eighteen. He wasn't bright at school and became a factory sweeper when he left. After the war was finished he became a delivery van driver, a job he kept until he retired at sixty-five. He appears to have achieved little over the years, and when you get to know him you discover that his whole justification for living is pinned to the fact that he was mentioned in war despatches. He clings to this tenaciously and proudly. It gives meaning to his life.

This kind of pride – which can occasionally lead to the glorification of war – needs to be handled very carefully. It may be the only thing that prevents the person from breaking down altogether as it usually conceals feelings of failure and worthlessness.

For others, the war was the only time in their lives which was filled with excitement, a time when their horizons were broadened beyond their wildest dreams and life since then may seem very dull in comparison.

Still others will feel guilty because they have lived whilst friends, neighbours, relatives died. This can lay a tremendous burden on people. As a result, some people have lived since then frantically trying to justify their lives, and burdened with guilt.

During any war many people go missing. Sometimes the authorities can confidently assume that they have died. But often families never know for sure and certainly never know where their loved one lies. Grieving then becomes very difficult, and is often not satisfactorily resolved. Again this can 'catch up' on people in old age and they will need help in 'letting go'.

It is a Christian's privilege to help people die at peace.

Coping with Dependency

Many people prior to death will experience a period of considerable dependency – either physical or mental, or both. At all times they must be allowed to remain as independent as possible and to remain in control of what is happening. Decisions should never be made for them unless they are mentally incapable of deciding for themselves. It is now legally possible to designate someone (with their full knowledge and consent) to cope with one's financial affairs in the event of one becoming incapable. It is called an 'enduring power of attorney'. The idea is to complete the form (obtainable from any legal stationers) and to lodge it with the Court of Protection whilst still fit and capable. When the designated representative feels the person has become incapable of managing their affairs they write to the patient, their relatives and the Court of Protection informing them that they intend to take over the administration of the frail person's affairs. If no one appeals within five weeks, they then become the legal administrator. More information about these 'enduring powers', as well as about ordinary 'powers of attorney' conditions, can be obtained from the Court of Protection.[2]

Increasingly, life is being prolonged by doctors through operations, use of sophisticated machinery and medication. Sometimes it does not result in an improved quality of life. The debate about euthanasia is likely to continue. Some people are now making 'living wills' which, whilst not having a legal status, do provide moral guidelines. In them people stipulate that they do not want resuscitation, lengthy attachment to life-support machines or life-prolonging medication when they are suffering from a disabling or terminal illness. The 'living will' is then lodged with the general practitioner and with relatives, so that the person's wishes are known if they are too ill to speak for themselves. More information about the powers of attorney and living wills can be got from your local Citizens Advice Bureau.

The issues about what does or what does not constitute euthanasia are far from simple, and although Christians are almost unanimous over deliberate decisions to end life, the situation is much more blurred when a person may or may not live without medication being given.

For anyone who wants to pursue this issue, there are books on ethics and morals which cover the issue generally. Here is an illustration of a common situation:

Doris, who has senile dementia, has not been able to look after herself for two years. She is not able even to recognise who her relatives are, and is unable to hold a conversation with anyone for more than five minutes, and even then much is incoherent. Her relatives are breaking under the strain of caring for her. She frequently gets chest infections for which the doctor gives her antibiotics. Each infection leaves her weaker and even more dependent. One day she gets pneumonia. Do you think she should be given antibiotics? What reasons would you give for your decision?

Bereavement

Public discussion of death and bereavement has not been common over the last fifty years or so. I suspect it is because death has become a much more private experience. Up to the last war there were clearly defined rituals surrounding death: the person probably died at home; a designated neighbour washed the body and prepared it for burial; the person was laid out in the front room and friends, neighbours and relatives paid their respects; curtains were drawn; black was worn for the funeral; men wore a black diamond-shaped patch on one arm of the overcoat for several months afterwards; the widow wore black clothes for a year and was not expected to join in 'happy' activities; the following year she wore sober clothes and gradually took up life again. All this ritual meant that everyone was constantly reminded of the fact of death, and people were given a symbolic structure to grief. These rituals gradually died out after the last war.

Experience of death in a meaningful way can now come for many people for the first time in middle age, with a concentration in old age. Another result of increased life-expectancy is that in previous generations it was unusual for death to come after thirty, forty, fifty or sixty years of intimate relationship. Death came before bonds were nearly so close. To be bereft of a partner after sixty years of life together is no longer uncommon, and is a devastating experience. It is a tribute to the maturity of older people that they cope so well. They are being asked to start a completely new life. How can older people be accused of being rigid and resistant to change?

There are three aspects to getting over a bereavement: coping with the feelings, the behavioural reactions and the practicalities.

Feelings

The feelings, which usually start with numbness, shock and a sense of unreality, cover most of the spectrum – intense sadness, self-pity, despair, fear, panic, denial, guilt, anger and bitterness, anxiety. When the dead person has suffered there can also be a sense of relief and when the person was a Christian the joy that they are now with the Lord. But even when God can be seen clearly at work in the timing of the death of the loved one, it does not mean that grieving is wrong. The pain of parting is the price of love. Some Christians want to deny this pain. This can lead to a faith that is falsely joyful. Another danger is that an unreal emphasis on joy can mean that the grief is not resolved in a healthy way. Sometimes Christians think negative feelings are dishonouring to God and a sign of faithlessness. Whether this is true will vary from person to person. But a confident and healthy faith only comes through testing and trials. So weakness always has to be acknowledged in order that faith can grow. Remember, too, that Jesus was a very 'feeling' person.

The depth of feeling varies according to personality, and in older people the feelings are often less violent. There are at least three reasons for this.

Where grieving is more familiar to them, they are more used to the feelings and so feel them less intensely. Secondly, even though there is a deep sense of loss, there is an acceptance that death in old age is to be expected. Thirdly, people also experience a sense of gratitude to God that the person lived so long.

An area of particular difficulty to elderly people who are widowed after a long, close marriage is the loss of affection. We need to remember that older people, who did not have contraceptive methods like the pill available to them when they were young, learned how to share deep intense feelings of love through extensive use of touch and intimate words. This does not usually diminish with age. If anything, it is likely to have increased, because of the once common but false idea that couples would seldom have sex after the woman's menopause. The loss of this deep intimacy by death can lead to intense loneliness. This can be aggravated by the widow or widower being unable to discuss their sexual loss with other people.

Behaviour

Emotion is not only expressed through feelings but also through behaviour. Common manifestations are aimless wandering and restlessness, talking to the dead person, or behaving in other ways as though he or she is still alive; loss of appetite; the aggravation of existing illness or the appearance of new ones; either disposing of all the dead person's possessions very quickly and indiscriminately, or keeping everything the same; refusing to see people; sleeplessness; impulsive decision making; loneliness; either inability to visit the grave at all, or returning obsessively; neglecting themselves and/or their home. 'Seeing' or 'hearing' the dead person is a common experience and many older people derive much comfort from it. (This is very different from deliberately trying to make contact with the dead person through seances or spiritualist meetings – a practice which is forbidden in Scripture.)

Many of these behaviours are common to all ages, but I want to comment on two of them. There is an increased risk of death during the year following a major loss – this is not surprising, as grieving puts an enormous strain on the body and mind and if the bereaved person is already frail it may all be too much. Secondly, it is usual for an existing illness to get worse at this time (although it may improve again later).

Practical Aspects of Bereavement

Death, particularly of a partner, also involves a lot of practical matters. To begin with, funeral arrangements have to be made. Whilst some people are content to leave arrangements to another relative or friend it is not wise for the closest relative to abdicate all decision making, although if the person is mentally frail it may be more a case of checking that they agree with the decision made. However, every effort possible must be made for elderly people, however physically or mentally frail, to attend the funeral, even if it means leaving hospital for the day. Failure to attend the funeral has been repeatedly shown to lead to severe complications later, and not infrequently leads to the complete denial of the death. This is particularly true if the bereaved person has a poor memory because of some illness. Whilst there is the instinctive wish to shield a person from pain or extra strain, in the long run it is cruel.

Another ill-advised, although instinctive reaction, is to feel that a widow or widower can no longer live alone. Decisions to move made quickly after a death are hardly ever wise, and if the bereaved person is very frail it is much better to try to arrange extra support for at least six to twelve months, even though it may involve the risk of a fall or self-neglect. I am sure that if Emma (see page 103) had moved when her niece died, either to an old people's home or to live with another relative, she would never have learned to care for herself. Of course, sometimes the extent of the care a frail person received from the dead person may not have been realised but even so, given that everybody functions less well while grieving but normally picks up later, it is impossible to make an accurate assessment of their capacity to cope at this time. Moving house quickly after a bereavement adds to the loss and creates extra strains; it also inhibits the natural grieving process and leads to all kinds of problems.

Soon after the death or funeral it is often helpful for the person to have a short break, but again it is better not to defer sleeping in the usual bed for too long.

When someone has lost their partner they are left with having to cope with all the jobs the other person did. In a generation where male and female roles were more clearly defined this can mean having to learn a whole range of new skills – cooking, shopping and cleaning for the man, business transactions like banks, payment of bills, electrical and plumbing repairs etc. for the widow – and all at a time when the emotional capacity is much reduced.

Most bereaved people will welcome someone willing to share their grief and listen to them when they are ready to talk, perhaps going over the same ground several, if not many, times. Strong feelings can be frightening, and expressing them to someone else can be comforting. It is important to reassure them that gradually the feelings will become less intense. However we need to keep a sensitive balance between encouraging the person to express their dilemmas and feelings, and not pressing them to share what they cannot or do not want to express.

A bereaved person may lay unjustified blame at the door of doctors or nurses, or there may be self-recrimination. This is natural, but gradually the person will see that the death was inevitable.

Often grieving people are avoided because of a fear of upsetting them – don't worry. It doesn't matter if they cry because you say something, but never suggest that they should pull themselves together; it takes months – even one or two years is not unusual – to get over the loss of a loved one. The gift of a suitable book of comfort can be helpful – Christian bookshops usually have quite a variety – and the sharing of relevant biblical passages.

Sometimes grieving people think their feelings are sinful; but they should be encouraged to express them to God, if not to other people. Buried feelings only come out in some other way. A person may feel that they should not be angry because they feel anger is a sin. However, if they feel angry it is better for them to talk about it or express it in some non-damaging way than to try to deny it because they feel guilty about it. The anger can be expressed to God either as a feeling or as a sin which needs forgiveness. Anger against God is a common reaction in bereavement and it is much better for it to be acknowledged to God. He is big enough to take it – even if repentance is right afterwards. Guilt, unforgiveness and regret can be coped with in the same way.

Practical support is sometimes necessary in the areas where they have problems; for instance a person who is not used to doing shopping may need someone to go with them several times until they get the confidence to cope alone. It may help to work out with them quick, easy, nutritious meals – especially using their favourite foods so that they are encouraged to eat even when they don't feel like it, or to take in tasty home-cooked meals or cakes for them. People who are unused to handling finances may appreciate an offer to go with them to the Building Society or bank, or to help them write the necessary letters, to fill in cheques, cope with pension books, etc. It may be necessary to go often over the same ground – learning for anyone is a *very* slow process when the mind is already in a turmoil. An invitation to a meal, to church and community activities – any change of surroundings – can help to prevent long term isolation, even if they are miserable. They should be encouraged to keep to their previous routine as far as possible.

If they have health problems, they should be urged to see their doctor. The illnesses are unlikely to be imaginary, and early help may prevent long-term problems. If sleeplessness is a problem – try to help them not to worry about it and find practical ways of coping – a flask of tea or chocolate by the bedside; a radio (with earplugs if disturbing other people is an issue) which can be tuned to the World Service or other channels that are on all night; moving the TV into the bedroom; the loan of books or tape recordings. If a person experiences restlessness, it is helpful to suggest some worthwhile occupation and perhaps do it with them. Be imaginative in suggesting new activities or people they might meet once the grieving begins to lessen – but do not provide stock ideas like old people's clubs or day centres unless you *know* these would be appreciated by a person. They only appeal to a minority of people.

Encourage them to talk about the happy memories they have of their time with the person who died, get them to show you photographs, etc., and use these as topics of conversation. Above all be sensitive, remind them that the black clouds will eventually lift, life will be worthwhile once again and God will have work for them to do. When they come out on the other side they will be stronger people with a deeper faith.

Multiple Bereavements

Whilst it is easy to be aware of the death of someone's husband or wife and therefore more helpful and understanding, less visible deaths can cause deep pain. The loss of close friends perhaps of almost a lifetime's standing, can leave a deep emptiness. So much has been shared. Where people make friends only with others of their own age group they will inevitably be very affected. They may experience multiple losses and because we do not know these friends and relatives we may not be as sensitive as we should be. People still need opportunities to express their grief. Sensitive, friendly enquiries over a period of months will help someone to feel that they are still important. Long-standing friendships cannot be replaced overnight, but we can gently help them build up fresh ones. All this should be borne in mind if a person seems moody, awkward or unreasonably resistant to change. Loss of any kind always leads to the need to conserve as much security as possible. It is entirely natural to resist all change that seems even remotely unreasonable or unnecessary.

Therefore when a change in the way things are done in church is proposed, maybe we should check out just how much change older people have had to cope with in their own lives recently and take this into account. Churches can do much to encourage relationships across the age range, and this helps people to be less isolated and lonely when friends die. Other relationships can then become deeper and richer.[3]

Part Two

CHAPTER 10

Primarily for Ministers and Leaders

The seeds of this book were sown over ten years ago when I had become increasingly aware of the negative attitudes about ageing and elderly people expressed by ministers of all denominations and in the religious press, and began to wonder how these had arisen. This led during the 1980s to a survey on the teaching about ageing given at all the major denominational theological institutions in England and Wales. Two colleges stood out. They each provided a teaching block on various aspects of ministering to older people (within their own theological perspective) and were at pains to stress the positive opportunities for ministry to this age group. Another two ensured that older people featured significantly in general teaching themes. At over half the remainder old people received no more than a passing mention, and at the rest teaching came in a module which focused on a secular theory of human growth and development and was covered in sessions coupled with death and bereavement! Talking to ordinands and young ministers today gives me no reason to think that the situation has changed significantly. A common excuse for neglect was that students found the subject dull and boring. (This is probably true because the teaching was always problem-orientated and depressing.) I hope this book will remedy that.

It is not surprising therefore that churches have ignored the needs of people in this age group. If this situation is to change, then it does require ministers to take a lead, as well as colleges to offer more positive theologically-based teaching.

If you are not doing them already there are some simple, non-time-consuming basic things which can be done to increase a positive attitude to older people.

1. Ensure that there is no public use of perjorative terms (like 'shut-ins', 'geriatrics', 'old biddies', 'old dears', 'wrinklies', 'little old ladies' and others), but that language is positive and affirming. When praying for sick people ensure that God is thanked at the same time for their gifts. Watch out for references to work and unemployment as so often they implicitly reinforce negative images of retirement.

2. Constantly question your attitudes to what you read. A while back a religious paper recorded that as 85 per cent of conversions occur to people under twenty-five, more evangelistic resources should be concentrated on that age group. The truth of course is that 85 per cent of conversions happen to people in that age group precisely *because* evangelism is already largely focused on them. If more attention was focused on presenting the gospel in ways applicable to people of other ages and therefore with different preoccupations, the conversion statistics would change.

3. Increase the congregation's awareness – including the older people themselves – of their own negative attitudes and what they unwittingly absorb through television and newspapers. When older people or issues related to them are mentioned in a Bible reading which is then being expounded, make sure that those references are not skipped over.

4. Check out, every so often, that every age group in the church is getting a reasonable share of your attention. Even if you are particulary gifted with another age group, e.g. young people, remember they will be influenced in their attitudes to older folk by how you behave. If you value everyone equally, then in time so will most (!) of the congregation.

5. Take an interest in those caring for a frail person; this in turn will draw their need to the attention of others.

Allocating Time

The demands on you as a leader are so heavy and time-consuming that it is essential you decide your priorities in service to elderly people. Who amongst the older people do you visit, why and how often? Obviously the number of older people in your church and in your community will influence your decision, as will the other demands on your time and the level of your own pastoral gifts.

It is inevitable that churches which develop ministries with older people will be making more demands on the minister simply because more will be known about their needs. The level of that demand will to some extent be influenced by the place of communion in the life of the individual and the church.

In Roman Catholic, Anglo-Catholic and Orthodox churches the Mass, or the Eucharist, is central to the life of the believer and this may also be true for some 'middle of the road' Anglicans. The practice has grown up in Roman Catholic churches of specially prepared lay people being licensed to take communion to sick or housebound members directly after Sunday mass. This is lovely for the sick person and eases the priest's load, but it then becomes very easy for the priest not to see these parishioners for a year at a time. Yet visiting them is important because many will have been used to going to confession regularly in the past. People who are not visited will tend to feel that the priest doesn't consider them important.

Similar problems can occur in churches where communion is not the centre of the individual's spiritual life. There is a tendency to forget that the weekly celebration of communion at evangelical Anglican churches is relatively recent. How often should communion be taken to people at home? Will you visit at other times as well?

Another issue arises around whether the Lord's Supper should be celebrated alone with the housebound person or whether others should also be present. Of course, if they are being regularly visited by a member of the congregation it would be natural for that person to be present too. But how about others as well? It takes more organising, and the service is bound to be longer, but on the other hand it gives a greater sense of the family of God meeting together. Might it too, in rural areas, provide an opportunity for some members of a village community to share communion more often?

Finally, some churches believe that the Breaking of Bread should take place either very infrequently and/or only when the whole church comes together. What does it mean for the housebound church member to be permanently excluded? In one church I knew which believed that communion was for the gathered church only, and which had a joint leadership of elders, one housebound member was never visited by the oversight during the last four years of her life, although a female member of the congregation visited regularly. This should not be.

Your Ministry with Older People

It is important, too, that your attitudes to visiting are thought through. Is it seen as a chore? Do you expect a stereotypical response from the people you visit? Do you think of them in a patronising way – or do you expect them to minister to you as well as you ministering to them? If God is constantly talking to each one of us throughout the day (and it is my experience that he is) then we should expect to be ministered to by them. If this doesn't happen, what might be wrong? Sometimes it can be because secular counselling methods have become such a way of life to leaders that ordinary relationships just don't happen.

Irrespective of the strengths or weaknesses of the psychodynamic non-directive methods of counselling, and their use with younger people, it is generally accepted amongst workers with older people that this is not the most helpful way of forming relationships with them.[1] They benefit from more concrete approaches. It is important that they have something to give to you and to the church, and an overly dependent role should be discouraged. One aim with older people is always to reduce their sense of helplessness and to encourage them to respond to external threats in an adaptive way, using the many strengths they have built up over the years. Affection for a priest will be a very important part in this process. At times the person who is getting frailer may need to be confronted with the choices they must make. The helper not trained in these non-directive counselling techniques will respond naturally but non-directive counsellors often either revert to an overly directive approach or seem to pussy-foot around. The frail person needs realistic assistance in co-ordinating the help they need or are receiving from family, statutory and voluntary agencies (doctors, nurses, meals on wheels, etc.) and in assessing accurately the available choices, so that they get the most satisfactory help to meet their need. They may need practical help in implementing their choice. For these reasons Christian counselling methods (eg Gary Collins, H. Wright, Selwyn Hughes) are much more appropriate. (Of course, people who are now elderly, who have consistently used non-directive counselling methods in the past, are unlikely to be open to the use of other methods with themselves. They are very difficult to help if they then become frail.) The minister, in counselling an older person must, on the other hand, remain objective and be willing to defend that person's choice in the face of opposition. The most likely time for this to occur is when neighbours are anxious about an elderly person's ability to continue to manage alone. Ministers need to be aware how much power is vested in their office, and therefore what they say carries an influence not held by a lay person. I have known several old people go into homes becaue 'their minister said they should' and then the outcome has not been satisfactory. Like so much in life a delicate balance is needed! Sometimes an older person will need gentle encouragement to move to an environment which can more easily provide for their needs, but at other times they will need encouragement to stand by their own decision to remain where they are.

However, do remember that your primary role is always spiritual, so whenever possible prayer, Bible reading and spiritual hope should be introduced. If you are visiting someone with no previous church connections it may not be possible to introduce these on a first visit, but you should be working towards it. I am increasingly concerned at the number of old people who remark about the minister's visits being social in character and who long for spiritual encouragement.

As a minister or church leader you also need to think through your relationship and policy towards other professionals. Sometimes social workers or doctors see churches as providers of voluntary visitors for lonely people within their area even when there has been no church involvement with the person in the past. Whether this responsibility can or should be taken will depend on many factors, including the size of your congregation, the number of people with the necessary skills and time, your church's attitude to evangelism, church priorities.

On the other hand, people you come in touch with may need a variety of services supplied through health, voluntary and local authorities, and there may be a network of contacts between professionals often involving the disclosure of confidential or semi-confidential information to each other. You need to think through very carefully the extent to which you should be involved professionally in this network.

A time when so many churches seem to lose contact with housebound, previously committed church people, is when a minister leaves; so often he takes his visiting lists with him! It would help a lot if ministers on leaving a church ensured that during the interregnum people were followed up by the laity and the list then handed to the new minister. Whether a minister enjoys visiting housebound folk or not, I do feel that new ministers must carry on the visiting system of their predecessors (if necessary introducing a different scheme later). I have met so many Christians, with a life's commitment to the church behind them, who are bewildered and upset when they lose touch with a church after they have become frail.

A crucial point of contact between the church (especially Anglican and Roman Catholic churches) and older people, is at funerals. There is enormous potential here for ministry. The undertaker is always able to give you information about the next of kin or the person arranging the funeral. Wherever possible a personal visit before the funeral is much appreciated by the bereaved person. A further visit two to three weeks after the funeral shows further care because it is then that neighbours, relatives, etc. have returned to their homes and normal lives. Yet it is at that point that the shock is wearing off. Many will say at this point that they are all right, but there will be quite a number, particularly of older folk, who will welcome a visit from someone from the church, and this need not necessarily be the minister. We know from surveys that losing a close relative or friend is an event that can lead (after a while) to a person going to church.

It often takes courage from anyone, particularly an older person, to find out what goes on in church. Many people have the most inaccurate ideas, and so if a stranger turns up in the congregation, particularly in old age, it really is of value to visit and get to know them. This may not be possible in a large church but it should be possible in smaller ones, even if after an initial visit a suitable lay person 'adopts' them until they feel at home. Perhaps in larger churches a lay person could take responsibility.

Introducing Change

As the work expands or situations change, you will want to introduce new things and end other activities. A popular stereotype of older people is that they will automatically resist change. This is not true, but what *is* true is that some people from every age group will be unhappy about the development. This can be minimised if change is introduced in an acceptable way and due attention is paid to people's attitudes and opinions. I am dealing with change here in some depth because I would like to suggest a model that ensures that older people do not become marginalised in the process.

Attitudes can never be imposed from above, and if people are to be committed to a particular change then they must have a positive attitude to it. I hope that by focusing in many of the earlier chapters on pastoring skills, changed attitudes in churches will come from people at the 'grass roots' as well as from leaders. This is always the least controversial and most effortless form of change. But this approach is not always possible or desirable. From my experience there are then a number of key issues to keep in mind.

First of all, build up a profile of the church. How has change been introduced in the past? To get at this you need to talk to a variety of people, particularly those who are middle-aged and elderly. Try to piece together a history of the church over the last forty years. How much change has there been in ministerial leadership in that time? What were the individual ministers' styles? What have been the number of baptisms, conversions, confirmations, etc., and what were the approximate ages of the people? Who are the key people in the church now? (This will not necessarily be the same as those on the PCC or the diaconate!) Have new Bibles, hymn books, chorus books, etc., been introduced? If so, when, and how often, and with what results? How much/many other changes is the church having to cope with at present? For instance it seems to me that new ministers frequently underestimate the extent of change they bring. Even when (although rarely!) they deliberately set out to keep things the same, the congregation will still have to get used to things being said in new ways, a different selection of hymns, a different set of people that he is attracted to, a different set of interests. Where a church is constantly faced with a mobile congregation the stable core will have less emotional and physical stamina to cope with other changes.

All change brings both losses and gains, and in preparing for change it is important to think through who is going to gain from the change, who is going to lose? Your own individual motives for wanting something need to be sorted out. Then the vision needs to be passed to others without them feeling pressured or 'hijacked'. Assess how much you are prepared to listen to the views of others. For the change to be really creative and 'owned' by the congregation they need to be involved from the start. It is good to begin by sounding out an idea over several months with a wide range of people – the more the better, and including those who are likely to be antagonistic. They often have useful points to make. Identify those with a ministry of intercession, get them praying deeply, and ask them to feed back to you the answers and impressions they get. Ask people generally to pray; write briefly about the idea in the newsletter or magazine and bring it in when appropriate in Bible expositions and sermons. Begin to identify people who might be involved; those who are antagonistic; those who are fence-sitters; those who will back it.

As the ideas get firmer, begin to list, in as non-judgmental a way as possible, the pros and cons that other people give to you, so that they can be presented to the church's decision-making body and eventually to the whole congregation. Your aim is to get as much support as possible for the scheme.

In an earlier chapter I talked about services in old people's homes. A church I know decided to develop this ministry. Like most churches, members were already involved in a lot of activities, and it needed careful 'selling'. They were able to build on the church's fundamental commitment to evangelism, but even so it would have been easy for the Sunday school or music group leaders to feel threatened that this new activity would draw people away.

The group also acted out another useful principle of change. They had an experimental service. Whenever possible, do start with a short-term experimental period. It allows flexibility in altering the parts that turn out to be less than satisfactory; it allows other people's enthusiasms to be rooted in reality; and it gives the opportunity for sceptics to reassess their position. An experimental period demands that the results are measured honestly by explicit criteria laid down in advance and made public. A leader's later attempts to introduce change will inevitably be sabotaged after a congregation has experienced goal posts being moved in order for a leader to steamroller through his or her ideas! Congregational trust in further change is also affected if a recent minister has tried the same tactic.

Do make sure that older people are involved at every stage of the procedure. It is a fallacy that older people are resistant to change. *Listen* to what they say and respect it; make sure they hear about developments as they take place, even if they are too frail to come to church, and/or are not directly involved. Put proposed plans down in writing, with as much information as possible. This allows people to go through it at their own pace, but it also has other useful functions: it helps to clarify thinking and planning; it prevents members from getting hold of the wrong end of the stick; and it creates openness.

As the planned development becomes operational, make sure that it is a matter of constant prayer, praise and feedback. Remember, it is as the change becomes part of the normal routine that the fence-sitters make up their minds. As one wants them to be favourably impressed, carelessness at this stage needs to be avoided. But care must continue to be shown to those who oppose the change; it is easy for them to feel left out. Of course, throughout it all, prayer has been the key; a praying church is far more likely to go forward in unity than a non-praying one – unless the leader and a few stalwarts run everything whilst everyone else takes little interest!

Developing Pastoral Gifts in the Congregation

Another major responsibility of church leaders is in teaching/training the laity in their Christian development, which includes the use of their gifts and their relationships with people they meet in their daily lives. God will normally give each church some people with pastoral gifts – if he doesn't, then the reason why needs to be discerned and rectified. But usually pastoring gifts need developing, and although much of this will come through practical experience some more formal meetings to develop skills and cope with problems may be helpful.

Early in 1991 the Scripture Union Training Unit (26–30 Heathcoat Street, Nottingham NG1 3AA) will be producing a flexible training package based on much of the material in this book. They also produce other training aids that help to develop pastoral gifts which are easy and flexible to use.

Retired Ministers

For ministers, retirement is an even greater upheaval than for most lay people; they have to leave their home as well as building an entirely new life for themselves. No longer are they the centre of everyone's attention, always being consulted, involved in the constant cycle of Sunday services (which stop for no man!), preparing sermons, coping with doorstep callers and telephone enquirers. The change is dramatic and all too often the church leaders of the area to which they move see them as a threat, so their skills are wasted. Ministers and their wives, when they retire, particularly need help and understanding.

Sometimes ministers want a complete change of life when they retire, but most would like opportunities to continue to use their ministerial skills. Indeed, talking to many 'younger' clergymen, the thing they look forward to in retirement is being able to do the things they enjoy without all the administration and bureaucracy! However, when there is a retired minister in the congregation it is easy to feel that they want all the interesting parts that make your job less mundane! This can cause friction and misunderstanding. Sometimes, too, retired clergymen are a threat because they are good at things you are not. They may have more time for people than you, and for sermon preparation. Freqently the situation is aggravated because the issues are not faced openly. Sometimes the skills they have to offer need to be shared on a wider church basis, covering for interregnums, holidays, sickness, etc. Sometimes the retired minister needs to be challenged to develop an area of ministry he had little time for previously – but please don't automatically press him into a ministry entirely with older people, either in residential settings or their own homes, unless that is what he chooses.

Sometimes a retired minister might develop an entirely new piece of church work. There are many opportunities – providing no one is possessive!

Another issue is that retired ministers frequently retire to an area where there is a surfeit of retired clergy, whilst inner-city, urban priority, and very rural areas who are starved of resources could use their skills and spiritual maturity very effectively. Perhaps church hierarchies could do more to make this possible.

Much if not all, of what I have written in this chapter will be obvious to those who have been in the ministry for years, but I hope it may be of some help to those who are less experienced, and that the book will help those who are at theological colleges.

Theological Institutions

When I did my research study on the teaching of ageing at the main denominational colleges I found that they faced a number of problems which this book aims to solve at the same time as being written for lay people. One was the amount that students need to know. Church leadership involves so many different skills that colleges felt very pressured about what to include and what to leave out of their student teaching programmes. Naturally they tended towards dealing with subjects about which there is a written body of knowledge. There is very little Christian literature on ageing, and what is available mostly takes a Roman Catholic/Anglo Catholic stance and is only of use to a few colleges. Christianity, unlike all the other major world religions, has no theology of ageing, so any teaching had to use secular material; this is inevitably deficient in meeting the spiritual needs of older people, and at points conflicts with Christian perspectives on solving day-to-day problems.

Nothing has been written for the non-professional on skills of working with older people, and so inevitably one of two assumptions was usually made: 1) that general non-directive counselling is suitable for use with all people of all ages, or 2) that old people's problems are so intractable that there is not much anyone can do about them.

I was surprised at the third problem I found. Most colleges gave no training in the giving of spiritual guidance, as they considered students were generally too young and inexperienced and that these skills would only come at a much later stage in ministry. Again, as I can identify no books of spiritual guidance for those working with older people, it meant that colleges were unable to prepare students for this work.

A fourth problem was a frequent sense of powerlessness in tutors, because of time pressure, to deal with the ageist attitudes of students. By the time I saw them they had been bombarded with numerous pressure groups promoting the 'isms' – racism, feminism, class, poverty, etc. Here was yet another.

A fifth problem was the frequent placements undertaken by students with hospital chaplains. Inevitably the students got sent to see frail, long-stay patients, generally in very poor quality institutions. They never saw the exciting positive work which many hospitals are doing. Instead they had reinforced all the commonly held negative attitudes. Yet the people they ministered to during these placements represent less than 1 per cent of people over sixty-five (or 1 in 600 of the general population!).

I believe there are certain things that students and colleges can do quite easily to meet the stimulating challenge of preparing to work with older church members. Issues raised in earlier chapters of this book are obvious examples. But in addition, recent church history can be given a human perspective by asking a retired minister to talk with students about it. Where students do a human growth and development module, the perspectives of older people should be obtained through students interviewing between them a number of really elderly people, and listening to tapes of older people talking about their own lives. When subjects like leisure, employment/unemployment (as well as euthanasia), are discussed in ethics, the perspective of retired people should be included.

In parish or secular placements students should meet not only the very frail, lonely, housebound/bedridden people, but also older people, both active and frail, who have a positive attitude to life and have met the challenges presented by retirement. Above all they should meet people who are still growing as Christians and who have much to teach them about spirituality in old age.

For those colleges who can give more time or who prefer to set aside a block of time, I would be happy to help plan a suitable programme. Throughout the Bible we see the struggle society had to respect and honour older people, how precious they were in the sight of God, and how he had special roles for them to fulfil. Today we pride ourselves, rightly or wrongly, on our vast superiority over those who lived in biblical times; dare we then pay less attention than did our forebears in the faith to what older people can give us, or deny our time and attention to frail people as they strive to finish the race that is set before them and to receive the crown of glory?

CHAPTER 11

Spiritual Issues of Old Age

Biblical Perspectives

We live in an age when the relevance of the Bible to daily living has been challenged in some quarters on the grounds that it was written in an entriely different historical and cultural setting. Others try to dismiss it because superficially it may appear to provide contradictory guidance. However, neither of these arguments can be justified when we look at what it tells us about ageing and old age. The Bible always stresses the uniqueness of each individual and recognises that, whilst God lays down principles and laws for our good, the way he works with each individual is always unique. Therefore he will always provide checks and balances. We can also expect God to speak clearly to us through the Bible about ageing and old age, because these are experiences that transcend historical and cultural barriers.

Through the Bible God provides us with direct guidance about how older people should be treated, and also about how we should live our lives when we are old. We do not find this as a set of rules such as other religions provide, but as principles lived out in the lives of actual people.

Sadly I have not been able to identify any Christian theologians or scholars who have studied in depth what the Bible has to teach us on the subject. The perspective in this book is therefore a personal one, but it is nevertheless true that the Bible has profoundly affected my approach to the study of ageing and my relationships with older people. When I started reading the Bible with the theme of old age in mind I had no idea what I would find, and have been surprised that so far I have discovered that the subject is mentioned in more than three hundred passages and at all stages in the history and experience of Israel and the New Testament Church.

There are references in the lives of many named people; there are biblical commands on how older people are to be treated; and general observations about old age; there is guidance on how elderly people themselves are to behave. Sadly, in this book there is only room to skim the surface of the subject, but I hope it will encourage readers to search the Bible for themselves.

A general principle that the Bible stresses is that all humans are made in God's image and are therefore equal, even though individuals will have different functions and different gifts. Elderly people are expressly mentioned in this inclusive way in two key passages in the New Testament. One is in the events surrounding the birth of Jesus. The Gospels mention that rich and poor, male and female, ecclesiastic and outcast, the young, and the old (represented by the ageing widowed Anna in Luke 2.36–7) met Jesus as a tiny baby. The second key event was during the Pentecost experience, when Peter quoted Joel's prophecy (Joel 2.18):

And in the last days it shall be, God declares,
that I will pour out my Spirit upon all flesh,
and your sons and your daughters shall prophesy,
and your young men shall see visions,
and your old men shall dream dreams . . .
(Acts 2.17)

Old people are therefore equal members of the Body of Christ and still have gifts from God to share with the Church.

But ageism and the attempt to marginalise older people seems always to have been a constant temptation. It lies behind the fifth commandment to 'honour your father and your mother', and the Levitical teaching: 'You shall rise up before the hoary head, and honour the face of an old man, and you shall fear your God' (Leviticus 19.32). If at that early stage of Israel's development despising the old had been unknown, then God would not have needed to give the injunction. And it is a theme that is picked up at various times in the Old Testament.

Paul, in his letter to the Ephesian church (6.2), also picks up on the commandment and points out that it is the first of God's commandments with a promise – the promise being that honouring parents will lead to a long life for the younger generation. This is logical, as older people have the experience and (should have!) the wisdom to guide the younger generation in the ways of God. I say should have because the Bible notes that not all old people are wise (e.g. Job 32.9)! However, wisdom is something that the Bible suggests comes with age as well as being a gift from God. Respecting old people includes listening to what they have to say and acting on their advice. Paul recognised that the older women could help Timothy in his leadership of the local church by advising the younger women in the care of their homes and families; in caring with humility for the sick and those in need; and in welcoming those needing hospitality (1 Timothy 5.3–10). In the Old Testament it was the old men who 'sat at the gate' (i.e. were the 'town councillors'!) and it is interesting to see the ways in which the views of the young and the old often conflicted – so reminiscent of life today! In 1 Kings 12 and 2 Chronicles 10 we have in vivid detail the record of one such conflict. The advice of the young men rather than the old was chosen by Rehoboam, with disastrous results – tyranny, civil wars, cultic practices, the final break-up of Solomon's kingdom and the loss of all the wealth he had created.

It is easy to see how following the advice of the older people led to a long life in biblical times. They knew only too well the effects of hot-headedness; they had learned caution the hard way! They also had much to lose through war and conflict. All that they had struggled for during their lives, including their sons, daughters and families, could be lost. Wars wiped out whole communities, and it is interesting to see how the biblical records of people living a long life usually coincided with periods of peace.

But while the Bible is positive about what elderly people have to offer it does not avoid the issue of frailty. As it describes the changes in people that came as they aged it often mentions a physical handicap – but it is always specific. This is an interesting insight into the Hebrew approach to old age, because often the details of the lives of individuals were obviously written up after they died. Today it is rare to hear a dead person's handicaps referred to specifically – so often it is global statements which can imply a far higher level of frailty than was actually the case. For example we know that Eli's problems were blindness and obesity (1 Samuel 4.18); that Jacob became blind (Genesis 48.10); King Asa had problems with his feet (1 Kings 15.23); David suffered from hypothermia (1 Kings 1.1–4) and Barzillai at eighty asked to be excused further military service because his hearing was failing and he had lost his sense of taste (2 Samuel 19.31–9).

The Bible writers quite clearly infer that people were to be given help in order to minimise the effects of their disease or handicap (1 Kings 1.2–5) and Paul gives instructions as to when financial help was to be given to elderly widows (1 Timothy 5.3–6). However, this help was always in order to allow them to continue to serve God and to be fruitful members of the church. It is the model of how we should help and support frail people. It must be provided in such a way as to enable them to continue to use their God-given gifts for the benefit of the whole community of faith.

What then does God say through his Word to old people themselves, and to us about our own old age? It is worth remembering that much of the Bible was probably formed and written, under the hand of God, by older people. The Wisdom literature (Proverbs, Job, Ecclesiastes) shows that the writers had a deep insight into life, even if the Preacher, the writer of Ecclesiastes, had become cynical and bitter. He provides a clear example of what can happen in old age when negativity and pessimism are allowed to get a hold of the mind. Some of the kings and prophets provide lessons in how sin, once it gets a hold, affects more and more of life. Behind the statement about Eli's fatness (1 Kings 4.18) is his long-term weak will and inability to discern when God was speaking (Samuel had to go to him *three* times before Eli realised it was God's voice).

Another major role of the older men was to ensure that the young men were trained in the knowledge of God and of his law. The Bible is full of examples of what happened when the older men were faithful to this calling and the disasters that came upon the nation when the younger men were led astray into the false paths of idolatory and egocentricity. Older people need to fulfil that same role today.

In our society it is not until after death that a person's 'last will and testament' is divulged, but in Bible times people gave their own 'death bed' speech, from which we can see they were generally very much aware of what was going on around them. Sometimes they could try and hold on to too much power for too long – for David this brought a fresh civil war within the kingdom. Refusal to relinquish office can still cause problems today!

The Levitical laws recognised that older people were likely to be less productive than younger ones; the taxes paid by people over sixty were reduced (Leviticus 27.7). However, the famous passage on old age – Ecclesiastes 12 – can rarely have been true. In biblical times it would not have been possible for someone to have survived long with that degree of frailty, and even today it only occurs where drugs such as antibiotics have prolonged life but not resulted in maintaining quality. Given the whole tenor of the book of Ecclesiastes, it could be that the author's attitude to old age stems from his own psychological problems, or alternatively (or as well) his only memories of people who had died in old age of that period immediately prior to death which is now known as 'terminal drop'.[1] Using Ecclesiastes as the basis of teaching about what normal life in old age should be like is full of pitfalls for the unwary, and when used considerable care needs to be taken so that unbalanced negative attitudes are avoided.

A more balanced view on old age can be found in Psalm 71, and in Appendix A I have suggested its use as a Bible study on old age. It gives younger people a vivid insight into the struggles that can come in old age and encourages older people to see their own old age realistically, for the Bible writers always expect spiritual growth to continue right up to death.

Paul is always challenging people to a deeper knowledge of God whatever their outward circumstances. Take, for example, the prayer in his letter to the Ephesian church (3.14–19). It starts with a request for the strengthening power of God's Spirit, moves on to Christ dwelling in hearts through faith; then to solid foundations in God's love so that it becomes possible to experience the incredible vastness of Christ's indescribable love which is necessary before one can be open to be filled with all the fullness of God. That has to be the aim for every Christian but, apart from some mystics, that final point is unlikely to be experienced before old age, if then.

Quite clearly God expects older people to remain a contributing part of society. Nowhere is there any indication that God gives permission for elderly people to withdraw in order to concentrate on themselves (as is the view of some Eastern religions, or as was the popular professional view of the 1950s.) On the other hand the frenetic activity that characterises modern Western society is not scriptural either. 'Be still and know that I am God' is just as essential in old age as at every other stage of life. It is the God-directed activity that comes out of the stillness and waiting that becomes the serene, purposeful power that gets things done (Isaiah 40.31).

Whilst God is an unchanging God, he is nevertheless always wanting to lead his people into new experiences and in old age this keeps them fresh and lively (Psalm 92.14) and able to relate with people of all ages (Jeremiah 31.13). Older people do not always realise the influence they have; their ways may be copied (for good or ill) and their advice seen as authoritative. I was with a group of young people discussing who they would like to be like – it was not TV personalities, it was not any of the well known Christian leaders whom they hold in high regard, or the historical giants of faith – it was a retired elder who quietly and faithfully and seemingly unnoticed carries out his duties and demonstrates an unswerving commitment to God and his Word. I am sure he is quite oblivious of his influence, which comes from a life centred on the stillness of God – much as I suspect Anna and Simeon were unaware of the influence they wielded in their day.

On the other hand, the stereotype of elderly peole being rigid and unchanging is, like all stereotypes, not without some truth. Job's ageing counsellors showed a total inability to move outside their previously well-proven theories and proved incapable of understanding or relating to Job in his troubles (Job 16). (Incidentally neither could the young Elihu, thereby showing that wisdom and the Spirit of God are not the automatic prerogative either of the young or the old!)

However, God expects nothing of us that he himself does not do. As he expects his people to care and support the older people who need it, he also specifically says that he will not forsake his saints (Psalm 37.28). He will go on ministering to them, so that their fruit in old age will be ever more abundant, and they may be able to demonstrate in their lives true characteristics of old age.

> Bid the older men be temperate, serious, sensible, sound in faith, in love, and in steadfastness. Bid the older women likewise to be reverent in behaviour, not to be slanderers or slaves to drink; they are to teach what is good, and so train the young women to love their husbands and children, to be sensible, chaste, domestic, kind, and submissive to their husbands, that the word of God may not be discredited . . .
>
> For the grace of God has appeared for the salvation of all men, training us to renounce irreligion and worldly passions, and to live sober, upright, and godly lives in this world, awaiting our blessed hope, the appearing of the glory of our great God and Saviour Jesus Christ, who gave himself for us to redeem us from all iniquity and to purify for himself a people of his own who are zealous for good deeds. (Titus 2.2–5, 11–14)

Meeting the Spiritual Needs of Older People through Group Activities

When everyone in a local church is expecting and looking to deepen their faith, old people will be challenged to grow also. Growth will come naturally through the 'all age' worship of the church, so where there are smaller groups for midweek activities such as Bible study or care groups, older people should be part of them – if necessary the group meeting in their home. At other times, and for some people, especially those searching for a faith or on the fringe of the church, a mid-week meeting aimed specifically at the older people can be important. People of the same generation, who have grown up together, enjoy doing things together and can share common concerns. Such meetings can be a time when the more specific challenges of old age can be discussed. For those whose lives have become more limited they can provide the opportunity for them to hear what God is doing elsewhere, with speakers and films about the Church's work at home and overseas. Lay participation in leading worship is something fairly new in many churches and some older people are nervous about taking part. Midweek services can provide a starting point. An old and interesting idea which has recently been revived in some churches is asking people to think of Bible verses or passages on a certain theme and then to share them the following week. For example, one week the theme was gardens. Several of the older people spent many happy hours thinking of where the theme arises in the Bible and then sharing their discoveries. A couple who live in a sheltered housing complex got other tenants involved in the Bible hunt as well! A Roman Catholic church has its mid-week group hunting up information about one or other of the saints whose festival is celebrated during the following week, and then sharing it at a Sunday mass.

Members of these groups can support each other during short-term illness and feed into the church the names of people needing longer-term support.

Nowadays, when fewer and fewer women of under retirement age are at home during the day, mid-week groups of all kinds tend to be dominated by older people who can still get about. One church, concerned about the lack of transport for less mobile people, approached their local social services department and now have the use of a minibus with a tail lift to transport housebound members to the group each week.

Alec said to me of the fellowship at his church: 'It is one of the most creative places of care in the area; it straddles the boundary between church and non-church. The members are some of the best agents for evangelism and of skills of how to turn into growing old.'

The leaders of the meeting need to ensure that the basics of Christian faith are regularly explored, as well as helping people to experience and develop whole new areas of understanding about God. It is important to avoid the meeting becoming marginalised in church life, and to make sure that the whole church encourages and supports the leaders.

In Chapter 1, I shared part of Rachel's life story. For the last twenty years she has been running a mid-week older people's group. In recent years it has got smaller and smaller and now no longer attracts new members – primarily because the current members are very elderly and frail. Yet there were many older people in the area who could have been drawn to a meeting. Sensibly, the church elders encouraged Rachel in her meeting, but developed another afternoon meeting, structuring it differently, so that Rachel neither felt hurt, nor that her ministry was failing (because it wasn't although it was only meeting a limited need). The result is that God continues to bless Rachel's group, and the other one is going from strength to strength and meeting the needs of more active retired fringe members of the church and those tenatively searching for a faith.

Evangelism

But what of older people outside the church? How can the joy and the challenge of the gospel be shared with them?

Essentially it is no different from sharing the gospel with people of other age groups. Nationwide, missions show that it is the one-to-one befriending and prayer that is the normal basis from which commitment springs. Older people will frequently recognise when the concern is not genuine, so there must be a willingness to really care about them. This may involve demonstrating concern about a physical or social need and making arrangements, where possible, for that need to be met. It will involve, if people are being visited in their homes, making sure that promises about dates and times of further visits are kept. Their previous experience of the church and other Christians needs to be explored. What picture do they have of Christianity? What do they know about Jesus? About God? What is their perspective on sin and guilt, which are common problems in old age? Their guilt, particularly, may have grown out of all proportion and may also have been aggravated by the teaching they received in Sunday school when young. There may also be a fear of death. This and other sensitive areas should not be avoided, but it is crucial to be very careful about how and when the issues are raised. Generally the person will indicate in some way if it is something that bothers them, or if a clear prompting from God is sensed, and then it is right to talk with them about it. There is no need to be rushed for time, so allow the person to fully absorb the Christian information before going on to the next point.

Often the person may already be listening to the radio service each weekday morning and/or looking at televised religious broadcasts. Far larger numbers of people tune into these than ever go to church – and many of them are elderly. Certainly, discussing the radio and TV programmes will provide much useful conversation material. For those who are active, invitations to church services – or more particularly the weekday or women's fellowships – may be appropriate.

They sould be encouraged to read the Bible. At this stage of their spiritual search it is more important for them to read a version that catches their imagination rather than the one they may eventually meet if they come to church. The choice of translations is a very personal matter; some will feel at home with the King James Version whilst others will find a modern translation more appropriate. Like Jane (see p. 21), they may also find it more vivid. The church may feel that it is appropriate to lend cassettes of Bible readings to those who find reading difficult for one reason or another. Genesis is not necessarily the best place to start, although if someone enjoys good stories then it could follow one of the Gospels. Other books that are easier to understand by those to whom the Bible is strange are Acts, Philemon, Philippians, James. In the Old Testament one can get an historical sweep as well as plenty to think about by reading, after Genesis, Exodus chapters 1–20, Numbers 9 onwards, Joshua, Judges, Ruth, Samuel, Kings and Nehemiah. Some people will find it helpful to be pointed to passages that deal with specific difficulties that they are having: the Psalms are particularly good in this respect as they can also help people to become less embarrassed about prayer. When the person is really interested, the visitor may like to suggest that both read certain passages between meetings so that they can discuss them together. Older people sometimes lack purpose and this can be a way of stimulating new interests. It is important to make sure that once they express an interest they regularly get a copy of the church newsletter or magazine. Passed-on copies of Christian newspapers or other publications may also bring pleasure and widen interests. A sensitive balance is required between being too low key in presenting the gospel and overwhelming people so that they feel pressured.

Individual Spirituality

Older people can be faced with all the same spiritual challenges as the rest of us but there is no room in this book to cover them all! I have therefore picked out those which seem to me to occur more frequently. However, space prevents me from doing much more than drawing them to your attention.

Prayer

People's experience of prayer at every age varies enormously but for most, like Jane, it involves far more silence. A mystical closeness often develops with age even if the person's spirituality in earlier life has been very different. Often people, particularly from an evangelical background, are anxious about this and there is the need to reassure them that it is very natural. Care needs to be taken over which books on contemplative prayer are given to them, as most are far too structured for the needs of older people. I often quote to them the words of a simple French peasant: 'I just sits and looks at him and he just sits and looks at me'. On the other hand, other older people experience the presence of God far less than they have in the past. Ronald Blythe, in his book *A View in Winter*[2] describes the experience of some monks of how all the energy, enthusiasm and life has gone and instead prayer has become an act of the will rather than one of sense and feeling. Lay people are sometimes helped by approaching prayer in a different way – using the prayers of others, or a liturgy of some kind, or the prayers of the Bible. Sometimes it is just a question of plodding on and walking by faith not by sight.

A few are called by God into a ghastly barrenness when all reality of God is removed. Of course this can arise because someone has deliberately cut themselves off from God through sin. But it can also be God's testing. The awareness of the devil and evil is sometimes

164

very strong, sometimes it is not. Only someone who has been through this kind of experience can really help. It was once described to me as 'walking across the Antarctic during a winter blizzard'. Again the most helpful things are to encourage the person to hold on and recall memories of times when God has been very real, to point to biblical passages with which the person can identify. Browse through books on prayer at your local Christian bookshop and you may find one that will be of help.

Retirement

In Chapter 3 I spoke about the emptiness that can be felt after retirement when an important part of life has suddenly been taken away.

The Bible has much to say about emptiness and impoverishment. Jesus 'emptied himself, taking the form of a servant . . . and became obedient unto death, even death on a cross. Therefore God has highly exalted him . . .' (Philippians 2.6–9). Several of the beatitudes in the Sermon on the Mount are concerned with emptiness – the poor in spirit, the bereaved, the meek, the hungry and thirsty, the pure. God cannot fill anyone who is not empty. Spiritually, at retirement God gives another challenge to many to be more deeply filled with him; either to live a life of greater obedience to him or to find other idols or selfish desires to fill the void. There is a fresh opportunity to seek God's will and to learn more of what it means to act within it.

As the void is faced, shadows of the past arise; where there is sin it needs confession and for God's forgiveness to be embraced; where there is pain, it needs to be acknowledged to God; where it involves joy and happiness, then praise and thanks to God; the future is frequently largely unknown – it needs to be given into the hands of God. The hollowness can gradually be filled by a new outpouring of God's Spirit, leading to a new freedom to live in the present. This in turn allows a person to live life more deeply, to feel more intensely, to share with others more fully, to respond to others more appropriately, and to accept change more easily as the invitation of God to grow more like him.

The role of the Christian friend or counsellor in this situation is to pray with and for them, that they may know God's will for the next step of their lives. It is important to remember that God is rarely in a hurry and so they may well need to wait what seems a long time to know what God's will is. This is a lesson we see in action through God's dealing with many Old Testament people. Our frenetic society makes slowing down very difficult and pushes people into activity in a way God never intended. It is a frequent experience that he uses retirement to help people relearn the rhythm of life that leads to service which is fruitful and rooted in the rest and peace of God.

Retirement is a time when many people look back over their lives. No one is ever completely satisfied with the life they have lived, and a Christian review will ultimately involve repentance for one's failures and acceptance of God's forgiveness. But it should also include much praise and thanksgiving as God's faithfulness is seen at work. It is usually easier to see, looking back, how God used apparently adverse circumstances for good, than to be aware of what God is doing in the middle of trauma and upset. Often people need to tell stories to another in order to be able to look at them in a more detached way, and a perceptive praying listener can show how God has been at work and also point to resentments and failures that need to be left behind and to areas in one's life where forgiveness and/or healing are needed.

Forgiveness
Some Christians find forgiving themselves and others relatively easy but even so it is surprising how often one

comes across an issue where grudges are still being harboured. For many older Christians the challenge to forgive is a real issue today. So many have not had any teaching on it and indeed some may have been taught by ministers that their anger or bitterness is actually justified. But Jesus was quite specific when Peter asked him how often he had to forgive anyone who had hurt or harmed him. And we know that Jesus replied, 'Every time' (Matthew 18.21). Central too in the Lord's Prayer is the line 'Forgive us our sins *as we forgive those who sin against us.*' For those who find forgiveness a hard battle it sometimes helps to ask the person to go back in prayer (i.e. in the presence of God) to the time when they were hurt, to remember the events as they happened. I usually find that there are a lot of negative feelings of their own for which they need to ask God's forgiveness. A lot of emotion usually comes out, and then they are able to tell God that they forgive that person or people for the wrong and to ask God to forgive as well.

When this is done thoroughly and honestly, a person will always find that either a great lightness comes over the scene, or they see Jesus somewhere in the event, or feel a sense of release.

However, sometimes after that the person needs to continue to remember that they have forgiven the other person, and refuse to allow any sense of vengeance to continue to have a hold in their life. The psalmists show us how hard it can sometimes be to maintain an attitude of forgiveness. For example the writer of Psalm 55 illustrates how it is not achieved in a moment; how the feelings can be expected to ebb and flow over a period of time, how it is easy to become obsessed by them; how they can colour attitudes towards other people. For the Psalmist starts by seeing enemies on every side and it is only later in the psalm that he acknowledges the true problem – the betrayal by his very close friend. The

Psalmist does not recognise forgiveness as an issue because that only becomes truly possible through the death of Jesus and his example. However he does rise to the level of knowing that trusting God is ultimately the only answer to coping with what life has done to him. It is an issue to which I find God constantly returns with those who genuinely want to do God's will in every part of their lives.[3]

The Spiritual Dimension to Suffering

Forgiveness can also be a factor in coping with suffering. Operations and treatments may go wrong, appointments be cancelled, services not be available or not able to provide exactly what is needed. When this makes people angry and frustrated it can turn to bitterness and resentment. Apart from the physical and psychological effects which just make the person less able to cope, spiritually the person inevitably distances himself or herself from God and blocks God from using the situation positively. Accepting what has happened, forgiving people who intentionally or unintentionally have caused problems or pain, does not necessarily mean a passive acceptance (although for some people in some situations that may be right), but it does mean that the person is then in a position to work alongside God in getting the situation solved in God's way. Their own energies can then be used in fruitful ways.

Another factor is trusting God. It takes long experience of God's faithfulness to be able to say as Job said 'even though He slay me, yet will I trust him'. And I have frequently found that when God asks someone for a deeper trust in him, there is a sense of insecurity which needs to be overcome. This is why recalling God's faithfulness in the past is so important. It is the reason why we should share far more frequently than we do our testimonies of God's faithfulness to us, and ask others for theirs.

We can help older people when God challenges them by asking them about God's faithfulness in their own experience, and by pointing them to biblical testimonies, for instance Paul:

> What then shall we say to this? If God is for us, who is against us? He who did not spare his own Son but gave him up for us all, will he not also give us all things with him? Who shall bring any charge against God's elect? It is God who justifies; who is to condemn? Is it Christ Jesus, who died, yes, who was raised from the dead, who is at the right hand of God, who indeed intercedes for us? Who shall separate us from the love of Christ? Shall tribulation, or distress, or persecution, or famine, or nakedness, or peril, or sword? As it is written,
>
> > 'For thy sake we are being killed all the day long; we are regarded as sheep to be slaughtered.'
>
> No, in all these things we are more than conquerors through him who loved us. For I am sure that neither death, nor life, nor angels, nor principalities, nor things present, not things to come, nor powers, nor height, nor depth, nor anything else in all creation, will be able to separate us from the love of God in Christ Jesus our Lord. (Romans 8:31–9) RSV

Paul had discovered this truth through personal experience. David in Psalm 56 gives us an insight into his own struggle and pinpoints a number of problem areas – powerlessness (verse 1), fear (verse 3), a sense of being trapped (verse 6), tears (verse 8), being churned up (verse 8). Notice that he is aware of and acknowledges the way he reacts naturally, and this is an essential first step. He provides the recipe for coping with temptation – putting himself into the hands of God, reminding God of how difficult he finds the tears and the feeling of insecurity. Nevertheless he knows he must carry on behaving according to God's instructions and thanking and praising him, so that whatever anyone does to him he can hold his head up in the presence of God.

Submission is another element. 'Why has God allowed this to happen?'; 'I've never done anyone any harm'; 'I've always done my best'; are oft-heard comments. People may feel they have earned the right not to suffer. There is a temptation to work hard to try to please God rather than to live by faith in his sovereignty and in the daily recognition that it is his grace and overflowing love that gives life. Where someone has tried to earn God's approval, tremendous problems can arise when suffering comes. On the other hand, if work done for God comes from an overflowing joy at the security he gives us through his unconditional love, then it is easier to accept that suffering is never purposeless. Some of the Psalms give us an insight into how the struggle to submit to God's sovereignty works out in practice. Although they are generally centred on betrayal by another human being, principles for coping when the suffering comes from an illness can easily be seen – Psalms 6, 31, 61, 71, 73, 86 and 109 for example.

Psalm 71 is particularly appropriate as it gives insights from someone who was himself elderly, which is why it is often called 'a prayer of an old man'. It vividly portrays the suffering that leads to freedom and the despair from which hope is born; it can be a great encouragement to older people in their own struggles. It is for this reason, and also as a stimulus to thinking about old age in the experience of the Bible, that I have suggested it as a Bible study in Appendix A.

Paul's experience is an amazing example of how it is possible for suffering to be used by God to bring about spiritual growth; therefore when he says that thanksgiving plays an important part, we need to take notice. When he wrote the letter to the Philippians he was housebound in a dark tenement flat, dependent on his friends for meeting the rent bill and his daily living expenses, yet he could say, 'Have no anxiety about anything, but in everything by prayer and supplication *with thanksgiving* let your requests be made known to God.' (Philippians 4.6).

It was in the midst of those conditions and in the light of all the suffering he had been through at other points in his life that Paul emphasised the importance of thanksgiving. The psalmists often do the same. Psalm 56 mentions praise and thanksgiving several times and the theme is developed in Psalm 34. It is important to notice that neither Paul nor David deny their problems and adverse circumstance but praise God in the midst of them. In standing alongside those who suffer we must avoid any sense of false triumphalism and help the person to avoid it too, but at the same time we need to help them see God's continuing care and concern and encourage them to thank him for it.[4]

People who are struggling with pain and suffering need others to stand with them. A lot can be learnt about how *not* to do it from Job's friends who had a happy knack of saying the wrong things at the wrong time in the wrong way! No doubt the primary reason for that was that they themselves had never known despair like Job's – or if they had, their suffering had been deserved. It can also be true that no one can help another to know freedom in the midst of their pain and agony if they are still bitter, resentful and unforgiving about any suffering they have experienced. God always gives us the choice to accept or rebel against what he allows to happen to us.

It is when all the factors – forgiveness of God and others, trust and submission, praise and thanksgiving, come together that it is possible, like Paul, to experience joy, and to be able to understand what Paul means when he goes on to say in Philippians 4.7: '. . . and the peace of God which passes all understanding shall keep your hearts and your minds in Christ Jesus.' To those who stand by watching and encouraging, the signs of a Spirit-filled life then become unmistakable.

Such a person is Annie. She was born in Guyana and came to Britain in 1964. She was a devout Roman Catholic but a few years ago, after a time in an Anglican church, became a Baptist. There, in spite of ill health, she is a great source of encouragement to others.

When I was a chambermaid I used to miss breakfast every Wednesday and slip out to mass. If I had been found out I would have been sacked. One day the priest ask me how I managed it. I say, 'The Good Lord look after me,' and he did until I retire . . . Sometimes there's some prejudice because I'm black but I don't think about it. One say, 'Go back to the jungle,' but I learned she hadn't got a job. I understand. But it never happens now. Everyone talk to me and I'm so happy here, even though ever since 1976 it's been trouble, trouble, trouble all the time: but I take it with a smile.

Many people wouldn't understand me. I have only one life. I don't get a pension; I never earned enough, but I have three meals a day and a telephone. I'm rich . . . In the morning I say my prayers to help me, everybody round me, neighbours, the whole world . . . Every Lent I fast for forty days. Just drink. I play tapes of hymns and choruses all day. God is so good to me. I'm so free and so happy.

APPENDIX A

Practising Skills

Friendships take time to develop and they cannot be hurried. This is as true of developing a friendship with someone of a similar age as it is of forming a friendship with someone of a different generation. At the root of all worthwhile relationships is an ability to communicate with others successfully. This involves being able to listen compassionately, understand what another person is is trying to communicate to us and to be willing to share ourselves in return – our hopes, desires, challenges, failures and skills. It will involve doing these things together as well as just enjoying each other's company.

However there are ways in which understanding and compassion can be developed. Listening is made up of a variety of skills – understanding the language people use, showing your interest, sensitivity to feelings, knowing when to share information about yourself and when to let the other person talk, helping someone cope with their feelings of anger, boredom, anxiety, distress, silence, joy, exuberance, happiness for example. It is worthwhile thinking through what bits in communicating with others you find easy and what you find difficult and then working on them. Friends can be very useful; you can practise some of the various types of listening together and either role play situations or go over events that caused problems and practise other possible ways of coping. You can also practise asking questions in different ways and see how the way a question is phrased influences the answer you get.

Radio and TV are good methods of checking out how much you hear and see. Record short extracts and see how much you pick up; replay and check. You can use video films by watching the pictures without the sound. This is a good way of increasing sensitivity as to what people are saying with their bodies – it isn't always the same as what they are saying with their lips! Games like 'wink murder' are also fun ways of increasing awareness. But with people who have a physical handicap don't underestimate the effects this will have on their mannerisms and behaviour. To some extent handicaps can be 'mimicked' artifically. Spending some time with a splint on a finger or thumb can give a little insight into the limitations of arthritis, or using only one arm and hand (preferably the one you use least) to appreciate the frustration a stroke can cause. Walking around the home with thick pieces of foam strapped to the feet gives an idea of how it feels to cope with any illness that makes people shaky on their legs. If there is someone who can watch and describe your mannerisms so much the better. You'll be surprised how silly you look! If you've access to a wheelchair ask someone to wheel you round the local shopping centre for an hour or so. And if you need to push people round in wheel-chairs at church try and get a physiotherapist or St. Johns/Red Cross worker to show you how to do it sensitively and effectively.

With all the changes that are coming in the health and social services and those that have come recently in social security you could get a social worker or health service officer to talk to a group about what is happening in your area.

A group of you could check out your ideas about old age by writing down and sharing the adjectives that come to mind when the words 'old age' are mentioned. I find there are usually far more negative than positive ones. You can help each other to improve your attitudes!

Or you could jot down together all the references to old age in the Bible that you can think of. I find three headings helpful: old people who are named and the descriptions of them when old; instructions about how older people are to be treated; and general statements about old age – there are at least 300 so there's plenty of scope![1] Some of these could be grouped together to form the basis of Bible studies. Psalm 71 gives a good introduction to a Biblical approach to old age. Some questions you could think about are: what does the elderly psalmist tell us about God's character? What is his experience of life, suffering, living out his faith? What are the negative and positive effects of reminiscence on his thoughts? In what ways do his feelings conflict with his faith and what is God teaching him through this? What does the psalmist teach us about the role of prayer and praise at every stage of life? What can you learn from the psalm about old age and how to prepare for it? The elderly writer of psalm 37 provides one of the most penetrating personal examples of how to cope with suffering to be found in the Old Testament. (Job is really more of a philosophical treatise and provides few insights into how to cope practically.) The psalm rewards careful study richly.

These are some ideas. Where there are groups of Christians who would like to spend a day or some evening sessions in thinking through these issues as they affect a local church, I would, subject to time constraints, be willing to help in putting together a programme. But if you decide to do some practice, try not to make heavy weather of it. Fun and laughter will help you relax and then learning is much quicker and more enjoyable.

Note

A general listening skills training pack is produced by Scripture Union called *Christian Caring* and available from their training unit 26–30 Heathcoat Street, Nottingham, NG1 3AA.

APPENDIX B

Some Voluntary Activities

Activities with People
Escorts – children, physically handicapped, mentally handicapped or ill people
Campaigning – e.g. Care Trust, Lord's Day Observance Society
Play helper – hospital wards, groups, nurseries, toy libraries
Probation volunteer
Prison visitor
Volunteer driving – hospitals, health centres, shops, outings, etc.
'Sitting in' to give relatives a break – children, mentally handicapped, elderly
Hospitals – ward volunteer, radio broadcasting, shop or trolley helper, church sick visitor
First aid
Public speaking – for voluntary organisations (e.g. Tear Fund), on hobbies and interests, Bible studies
Promoting voluntary organisations – e.g. Tear Fund, Bible Society
Teaching – reading, numeracy
Door-to-door evangelism
Short term missionary service
Community Association involvement

Working for People
Braille transcribing
Recording special books for blind students
Fund raising
Typing and administrative jobs

Activities with Nature and History
Archaeology
Bell ringing
Recording – tombstones, memorials, old buildings, sites, etc.
Flower arranging
Nature observation and recording – birds, butterflies, insects, flowers, animals
Genealogies
Historical societies
Waterway restoration – maintenance, stewarding
Country house stewards and guides
Church and cathedral guides
Railway societies
Nature wardens
Conservation and restoration work – houses, environment, churches, etc.

APPENDIX C

Services Provided Through Health or Local Authorities for People in their Own Homes

The way health and social services are organised is going to be changed in April 1991. At present it is difficult to know how these changes will affect older people.

If you feel that an older person you know might benefit from one or more of the following services and you don't know how to find out exactly how it is organised or what is provided in your locality, the Citizens Advice Bureau should be able to tell you. Whilst it is a good idea for you to have detailed information to give to an elderly person about a service that they might find helpful, it is never right to give that person's name without their prior knowledge and consent to any service or individual. It is important, too, that you give any information to the elderly person in such a way that they don't feel obliged to follow it up.

Community Health Services

Access to most of these is through the person's doctor, although the *Practice-Nurse* where there is one, is frequently a mine of information. She (or he) carries out routine procedures on the doctor's behalf, like injections, dressings, screening. Her duties are similar to the *District (or Community) Nurse*. She visits people in their own homes, undertaking the nursing procedures outlined above, showing relatives and other carers how to nurse sick relations, supervising auxiliary nurses and bathing attendants.

Every area should have nurses who aim to keep abreast of developments in more specialised fields. For example every area should have an *Incontinence Adviser* who can give individual personal advice to people with toilet problems, can arrange where necessary for incontinent laundry services to be made available (sometimes arranged in conjunction with social services departments) and for supplies of pads.

Other specialist nurses may be concerned with the needs of cancer patients (often in conjunction with MacMillan nurses or home services organised by a local hospice) or with people who have a 'stoma' (i.e. an artificial opening through which the body's waste products are excreted).

The *District Nursing Service* should also be able to supply nursing aids like commodes, bedpans, back rests, etc. – sometimes in conjunction with the British Red Cross Society.

If a person needs a *wheelchair* permanently, then the doctor can order it, but if it is just needed temporarily, either the local Red Cross branch or the Social Services Department should be able to help.

176

Chiropodists, when employed by the health service, usually work at health centres on a sessional basis. Appointments can be booked without referral from a doctor. Chiropodists are in very short supply in some areas of the country so there can be a long wait for an appointment. A chiropodist may also operate privately. It is then advisable to choose someone who carries the letters SRCh after their name. Anyone can set up a chiropody practice and although some unqualified chiropodists are very skilled and experienced, many are not.

There are other community health care professionals who are usually privately employed and the NHS reimburses consultation fees for the NHS work they undertake.

The *pharmacist* who dispenses prescriptions ordered by the doctor is often an invaluable source of advice for treatment of minor ailments and can often answer questions about the side effects of drugs.

Ophthalmic opticians work primarily in private practice. Elderly people receiving income support and with little savings can get vouchers to help with the cost.

Dentists too are self-employed. The NHS changes a fee for dental inspections under the NHS and a scale of charges is imposed for treatment. For those with minimum savings receiving income support, as well as others on a very low income, an application for reimbursement can be made but it is essential to get a receipt from the dental receptionist. It is increasingly difficult to find dentists who will prescibe dentures under the NHS as they feel they are not adequtely reimbursed for the amount of work involved. The local Community Health Council (the Citizens Advice Bureau can provide their name, address and telephone number) should be able to tell you which dentists are prepared to help.

Community Psychiatric Services

Increasingly there are specialist teams who support people in the community with mental health problems. A *psychiatrist* is always in charge. Helping the psychiatrist may be *psychologists*, who with older people are usually responsible for the detailed testing of their mental capacities; it is from these assessments that it is possible to work out when a person has a long-term organic disease and when they have depression, or where both are present. They often also help by introducing people to behavioural and cognitive therapy. *Community psychiatric nurses* visit people regularly in their own homes and are often an enormous support to relatives in giving practical advice on a whole range of problems that arise when a person has a more intractable mental health problem.

Social Services Departments

Under the new legislation it is possible that even more of their services will be contracted out to private and voluntary agencies than in the past. However the social services office serving the locality in which the old person lives will continue to be the best place to start enquiries.

Home Care Service. The *Local Organiser* assesses what the person needs in terms of help with shopping, cleaning, washing clothes, meals, lighting fires, personal help with washing, dressing, emptying the commode. There is always a very heavy demand for the services so the organiser will seek to find other people to take on jobs! It is therefore very important that as a visitor you make it clear to the elderly person what you can and cannot do. For example in a country area shopping can be very time-consuming and she will often press the elderly person to find a friend or relative to do it instead. The *Day Care Organiser* is also frequently responsible for recommending people for meals on wheels, even where this is run by a local voluntary group.

Lunch Clubs and Day Centres. These cover anything from a place which can be used like a cheap restaurant through to specially designed centres providing facilities for people who are very handicapped and immobile and need transport to get them there. Normally a social worker will assess what the person needs. Apart from the cities, lunch clubs and day centres for active or mildly handicapped people are usually provided by voluntary groups.

Social Workers. Unless they specialise in work with older people they are generally preoccupied with undertaking work with families, children and mentally handicapped people as specified in various Acts of Parliament. But where there are specialist social workers they will help with a variety of problems – financial, mental health, housing, etc. Local authorities provide some residential care and social workers or their assistants assess people for this service where financial assistance is required. Residential social workers are normally in charge of homes and may also be involved in the assessment for care.

Occupational Therapists working for the Social Service Department provide for people who are phyhsically handicapped, through the provision of aids like walking sticks and frames, bath aids, pick-up sticks and reading aids. They also recommend adaptations to the homes of people who are severely handicapped. For example, if a person has to move around their home in a wheelchair, the toilet may need adapting, or a ramp be needed to the front doorstep. They can provide advice on how to adapt clothing, kitchen utsensils and many other household items to meet individual problems. If someone has difficulties because of a physical handicap it is well worth asking the Social Services area office if an occupational therapist can visit to discuss the problems and possible solutions. It is always better to do this than to go and buy aids privately without professional advice. They may also be able to lend suitable aids.

Library Service

Local libraries usually provide a home book service for people who cannot get out.

Voluntary Organisations

In most areas of the country there are also voluntary organisations which provide help for frailer people. These services frequently depend on volunteers and aim to meet local needs, so they vary enormously in what they provide. The Citizens Advice Bureau or local reference library is the best source of information about them. Some specialist national organisations (e.g. for Parkinson's Disease) may be able to refer you to a local branch of the organisation.

APPENDIX D

Some Voluntary Organisations

This is a list of some organisations which may be of help to older people and their carers. It is far from complete! A useful directory of organisations concerned with particular diseases and handicaps and which should be in your local reference library is *Self-help and the Patient*. It is produced and regularly updated by the Patients' Association.

Age Concern England 60 Pitcairn Road, Mitcham, Surrey CR4 3LL provide a wide range of services. Their information department is developing an extensive range of books and fact sheets on specialised areas, State financial benefits, income tax, e.g. *Building Society Interest, Income Tax, Housing Problems*. Write requesting a list of their fact sheets and publications which are available through booksellers, enclosing a stamped addressed envelope. The Insurance Officer can provide information about their various home insurance schemes – but alternative quotes should be obtained locally as they are not always the bst buy. Age Concern also has local autonomous groups mainly run by volunteers except in the large cities where paid staff are employed. The extent of their service varies enormously.

Alzheimer's Disease Society 158–160 Balham High Road, London SW12 9BM provide information, research and have local groups for carers.

Arthritis Care, 6 Grosvenor Square, London SW1.

Carers National Association, 29 Chilworth Mews, London W2 3RG. An organisation, with many local suport groups, which seeks to represent the needs of all those supporting frail relatives of all ages.

Centre on Environment for the Handicapped, 35 Great Smith Street, London SW1 provide technical information and architectural advice about the needs of handicapped people in relation to access to all parts of buildings and mobility in public places.

Colostomy Welfare Group, 38–39 Eccleston Square, London SW1V 1PB. Similar groups also exist for people with ileostomies and urostomies.

Consumers' Association, 2 Marylebone Road, London NW1 publishes many books available through booksellers, which provide practical information. They also publish the magazine *Which.* Their publications should be available in local reference libraries.

Disabled Living Foundation, 380 Harrow Road, London W9 have an extensive permanent exhibition of aids, and also produce publications and pamphlets on the various aids to assist disabled people.

Dial UK, 117 High Street, Clay Cross, Chesterfield, Derbyshire S45 9DZ provides information and advice for disabled people and their families through people with a direct experience of disability.

National Listening Library, Freepost, 12 Lant Street, London SE1 1QH provides cassettes and special reproducers which can be operated by handicapped people either manually or by remote control. Applications for membership need a letter of support from a doctor.

Parkinson's Disease Society, 36 Portland Place, London W1 3DG.

Royal National Institute for the Blind, 224 Great Portland Street, London W1.

Royal National Institute for the Deaf, 105 Gower Street, London WC1.

VOCAL, 336 Brixton Road, London SW9. A co-ordinating agency for a large number of organisations concerned about specific speech difficulites. They can put you in touch with the right individual or organisation to meet the need.

SPOD, 286 Camden Road, London N7 0BJ gives advice for those experiencing sexual problems because of physcial handicap.

Royal Association for Disability and Rehabilitation, 25 Mortimer Street, London W1 provide a wealth of pamphlets and information on all aspects of disability. They should know if a specialist organisation exists for a particular disability as well as being able to give addresses and telephone numbers.

National Federation of Housing Associations, 175 Grays Inn Road, London WC1.

Counsel and Care for the Elderly, 16 Bonny Street, London NW1.

The Shaftesbury Society, 2A Amity Grove, London SW20 0LH.

APPENDIX E

A Selection of Organisations providing Residential Care for Older People

Aged Pilgrims Friend Society, 175 Tower Bridge Road, London SE1 2AB. Sheltered housing and residential homes for elderly evangelical Christians.

Church of Scotland Board of Social Responsibility, 121 George Street, Edinburgh EH2 4YN.

Church Army Sunset and Anchorage Homes, CSC House, North Circular Road, London NW10 7UG.

Essex Federation of Congregational Women's Homes Ltd, Glebe House, Spring Lane, Leyden, Colchester, Essex. (Church recommendation essential. Only for men and women in reasonable health.)

Field Lane Foundation, (Christian Organisation), 16 Vine Hill, London EC1R 5EA.

Methodist Homes for the Aged, 11 Tufton Street, London SW1P 3QD.

Quaker Social Responsibility and Organisation, Friends House, Euston Road, London NW1. Sheltered housing and residential homes for active people.

Salvation Army (Women) 280 Mare Street, London E8 1HE; (Men) 110–112 Middlesex Street, London E1.

Please note that this list contains only a selection of agencies providing residential care. Some Anglican religious communities run homes and these are listed in *The Church of England Yearbook*, under 'Religious Communities'. Similar Roman Catholic homes can be found *The Catholic Directory* under 'Catholic Adult Institutions in England and Wales'. Copies of both books should be available in local reference libraries.

Inclusion in this list does not constitute a recommendation and applicants must satisfy themselves that any particular home can meet their needs in both the short and long term.

FURTHER READING

In addition to works mentioned in the Notes, I recommend:

Growing Older: Years of Fulfilment by R. Kaustenbaum, A Life Cycle Book (Harper and Row, 1979). An easy to read (secular) overview of old age, writen by an eminent American geriatrician.

Working with Older People: Open University Course P564. (Open University Press, 1990). An expensive but stimulating distance learning pack which encourages learning about old age through the direct experiences of elderly people and their helpers. Written in an easy non-intellectual style with many audio tapes which makes it an enjoyable learning experience.

NOTES

PART ONE

1   OLD AGE IN THE TWENTIETH CENTURY
1   An excellent article which discusses the strengths and weaknesses of the theories in more depth can be found in 'Approaches
to the Study of Ageing': Paper 5 by Christina Victor in *Mental
Health Problems in Old Age: A Reader*, ed. Brian Gearing, Mal-
colm Johnson and Tom Heller (John Wiley and Sons, 1988).
2   The information in this section is drawn from the following
sources: *Beyond Three Score and Ten*, Vol. 1 by Mark Abrams
(Age Concern England, 1978). *The Elderly at Home* by Audrey
Hunt (HMSO, 1978). 'A study of Religious Attitudes of the
Elderly' by W.S. Reid, A.J.J. Gilmore, G.R. Andrews and
F.I. Caird, in *Age and Ageing*, Vol. 7 No. 40 (1978). 'The Supportive Network: Coping with Old Age' by G.C. Wenger, National Institute of Social Worker Library No. 46 (Allen and
Unwin, 1984). Unpublished research by P. Coleman, Depart-
ment of Medicine, Southampton University 1978.

2   SPIRITUAL DIMENSIONS TO AGEING
1   Unpublished research by P. Coleman, Department of Medicine,
Southampton University 1978.

3   RETIREMENT – A TIME FOR NEW GROWTH
1   For example books by Selwyn Hughes in the Christian Counselling Series (Marshall). Books by John White (IVP). *Facing Anxiety and Stress* by Michael Lawson (IVP 1986). *Problems of
Christian Discipleship* by J. Oswald Chambers (now out of print,
but excellent if you can get it.

4   THE CONTRIBUTION OF OLDER PEOPLE
TO THE CHURCH
1   For instance, *Discovering your Place in the Body of Christ* by
Selwyn Hughes (Marshalls, 1982). The Anglican diocesan
advisers on stewardship have produced a wide variety of ques-
tionnaires – though elderly people are often seen as needing help
rather than giving it!

5   THE CHURCHES' CARE OF OLDER PEOPLE
1   When you are planning major adaptations, ramps or new buildings which involve architectural plans it is important to think in
detail about the needs of handicapped people. You can get very
helpful advice from the Centre on Environment for the Handicapped, 35 Great Smith Street, London SW1.

2 Impartial advice about the induction loop system can be obtained from the Royal National Institute for the Deaf, 105 Gower Street, London WC1E 6AH.

3 This is administered by the Christian Music Association, Glyndley Manor, Stone Cross, Pevensey, East Sussex BN24 5BS, from whom you can get full details.

6 MOVING HOME
1 See Appendix D for further details about Age Concern England.

7 FRAILTY AND SICKNESS
1 *A Step Further* by Joni Eareckson and Steve Estos (Marshalls, 1979).

8 MENTAL HEALTH AND ILLNESS IN LATER LIFE
1 *Masks of Melancholy* by John White (IVP). Chapter 8 of *Self-Talk, Imagery and Prayer in Counselling* by H. Norman Wright (Word, 1987).

2 A book written from a secular viewpoint which provides a lot of practical suggestions about coping with 'dementia' or Alzheimer's Disease is *The 36-Hour Day* by Nancy L. Mace and Peter Robins MD (Age Concern England, 1987).

3 Those who are particularly interested in mental health in later life, and have the time, may find a short Open University course designed for social workers, nurses, carers and doctors interested and stimulating. It is called 'Mental Health Problems in Old Age'. Further details can be obtained from the Department of Health and Social Welfare, Open University, Walton Hall, Milton Keynes MK7 6AA. In the pack there is a book of articles (with the same title) which is available separately and which can be borrowed from your local public library. (See Note 1 of Chapter 1 for the full reference.)

9 DYING, DEATH AND BEREAVEMENT
1 Corrie ten Boom had to struggle to forgive the cruelty of her German captors, and people may be helped by reading her *Amazing Love* (Christian Literature Crusade, 1953), as well as her other books. Two more particularly helpful books on forgiveness are *Forgive and Forget* by Lewes Smedes (Triangle, 1984) and *Caring Enough to Forgive* by David Angsberger (Herald Press, 1981).

2 Court of Protection, 24 Kingsway, London WC2.

3 Other books about death and bereavement which you and/or a grieving person may find helpful are: *A Grief Observed* by C.S. Lewis (Faber, 1961). *Facing Death* by Billy Graham (Word, 1987) *Facing Loneliness* by J. Oswald Chambers (Highland Books, 1988). *Learning to Walk Alone* by Ingrid Trobisch (IVP, 1986). The only piece of research about dying and bereavement in old age that I know of is *Life After Death: A Study of the Elderly Widowed* by A. Bowling and A. Cartwright (Tavistock Publications, 1982).

PART TWO

10 PRIMARILY FOR MINISTERS AND LEADERS
1 'Mental Health' by Professor Klaus Bergman – Chapter 8 of *An Ageing Population*: Open University Course P252 (Open University Press, 1979). Suitable secular counselling methods with older people are extensviely covered in *Mental Health Problems in Old Age*: Course 577 (Open University Press, 1988; and see above, Note 3 to Chapter 8). An excellent although expensive handbook for those able to use an electic counselling approach (although there will be the need to modify the approaches in the light of scriptural principles) is *Counselling the Ageing: An Integrative Approach* by Edmund Sherman (Free Press, New York, 1982).

11 SPIRITUAL ISSUES OF OLD AGE
1 'Terminal drop' is a medical term referring to the period of time prior to death when metabolic changes take place in the body. It is often difficult to spot at the time. However, looking back after the person has died it is often easy to see how they changed in the months before their death. Often a person becomes lethargic, everything takes greater effort, sometimes they seem rather depressed, often they want to sleep more and take 'cat naps' when that has been out of character.
2 *A View in Winter* by Ronald Blythe (Penguin, 1981).
3 See Note 1 of Chapter 9.
4 Two books which deal with suffering in a very practical way but from very different perpsectives are *The Suffering and the Glory* by David Prior (Hodder and Stoughton, 1985); and *Why, O Lord: The Inner Meaning of Suffering* by Carlo Carretto (Darton, Longman and Todd, 1986).

APPENDIX A – PRACTISING SKILLS
1 For those who would like to look a little more deeply at some of the Bible references, here are some to start with:
References to old people and their capacities include: *Lot* (Genesis 19.31); *Abraham* (Genesis 24 and 25); *Isaac* (Genesis 27.1); *Joseph* (Genesis 50.24); *Aaron* (Numbers 20.28 and 33.39); *Gideon* (Judges 8.32); *Samuel* (1 Samuel 8.1 through to 25.1); *Jesse* (1 Samuel 17.12); *Solomon* (1 Kings 11.4); Ahijah (1 Kings 14.4); *Jehoiada* (2 Chronicles 24.15).
References to wisdom and old age include: Deuteronomy 32.7; Job 12.12–13; Job 15.10; Job 32.6–7; Proverbs 20.29.
References about disrespect include: Exodus 21.15, 17; Leviticus 20.9; Deuteronomy 27.16, 19; Deuteronomy 28.50; Proverbs 30.17; Isaiah 3.5; Isaiah 47.6; Lamentations 5.12; Ezekiel 22.7.